Every Child
Welcome

*A Ministry Handbook for
Including Kids with Special Needs*

Every Child Welcome

A Ministry Handbook for Including Kids with Special Needs

Katie Wetherbee & Jolene Philo

Kregel
Ministry

Every Child Welcome: A Ministry Handbook for Including Kids with Special Needs
© 2015 by Katie Wetherbee and Jolene Philo

Published by Kregel Publications, a division of Kregel, Inc., 2450 Oak Industrial Dr. NE, Grand Rapids, MI 49505-6020.

All Scripture quotations, unless otherwise indicated, are from The Holy Bible, English Standard Version® (ESV®), copyright © 2001 by Crossway, a publishing ministry of Good News Publishers. Used by permission. All rights reserved.

ISBN 978-0-8254-4350-3

Printed in the United States of America
19 / 5 4

To those who were my students during my teaching career:
You taught me more than you will ever know.
~Jolene

To my wonderful parents, Mary and Barry Livingston,
who faithfully took me to Sunday School and who were
always certain that one day, I would write a book.
~ Katie

Contents

Introduction

Jesus sets a high standard in Matthew 19:14 when He says, "Let the little children come to me and do not hinder them, for to such belongs the kingdom of heaven." His invitation is inclusive. No gender is specified. The call is not limited to children who will sit quietly at His feet and listen, color between the lines, raise their hands and wait to be called upon, or who work at grade level. No child is disqualified because of preexisting physical conditions, mental illness, or behavior issues.

Jesus sets a high standard that can be difficult for children's ministry volunteers with willing servant hearts, but without professional child development or educational training, to attain. Difficult, but not impossible. Because when God issues a command like "Let the children come unto me," He equips people with willing, servant hearts to carry out His will.

Our Parenting Stories

We know this to be true because we are parents of kids with special needs. Katie's daughter, Annie, had a stroke at the age of five as the result of a rare circulatory disease. The damage to her brain caused right-sided paralysis. Annie also lost her ability to speak. Treatment involved a ten-hour brain surgery and years of physical, occupational and speech therapies, which helped her to regain her strength and language.

Jolene's son, Allen, had surgery for a life-threatening esophageal birth anomaly less than twenty-four hours after he was born. Complications led to six more surgeries before he was five and a final surgery at age fifteen. He then lived with undiagnosed post-traumatic stress disorder (PTSD), caused by early, invasive medical treatment. The condition was diagnosed and successfully treated when he was a young adult.

How do we know God equips those He commands to do His will? Because neither of us felt qualified to train up our children with special needs as parents are commanded to do in Proverbs 22:6: "Train up a child in the way he should go; even when he is old he will not depart from it."

Even though we didn't feel qualified—to be honest, we felt young, scared, ignorant, overwhelmed, and unqualified—God equipped us to carry out his command. He gave us everything we needed to raise our children . . . who are now young adults.

God's Equipping

We met at a special needs ministry conference in Des Moines, Iowa in 2010. Katie conducted a workshop to help pastors and ministry volunteers understand and include families affected by disabilities. Jolene was there to sit at her book table—hopefully to sell copies of her first book for parents of kids with special needs—and to attend Katie's workshop.

Katie made a beeline to the book table and introduced herself. Jolene had attended Katie's workshop and loved what she had to say. Before the end of the conference, we exchanged email addresses and quickly became good friends. Maybe because we had a lot in common. After all, we were both parents of kids with special needs. We were both former public school teachers. We both had special education backgrounds. We shared a similar philosophy about inclusive education. And we discovered that though we had taught in different states, we had employed many of the same strategies to create inclusive classrooms for our students.

In emails and phone calls, we often brainstormed about how to equip children's ministry volunteers to create inclusive environments for kids with special needs. One of our ideas was to create a resource full of simple strategies volunteers could use to make a variety of children's ministry settings more inclusive and accessible for kids with special needs. That idea birthed this book.

The Goal of this Book

Because children's ministry workers are volunteers who may or may not have training in the field of special needs education, one goal of *Every Child Welcome* is to encourage quality teaching. The goal is accomplished when volunteers assess and understand each child's strengths and needs rather than focus on the child's diagnosis.

Why did we choose this goal? Because it follows the example of Scripture. Throughout the Gospels, Jesus interacts with people who are affected by physical and mental illnesses in the context of their strengths and their needs rather than in the context of a diagnosis. In 2 Corinthians 12:7, Paul refers to his own personal weakness, perhaps what today would be called a special need, as "a thorn in the flesh." Instead of giving a specific diagnosis, Paul says, "Three times I pleaded with the Lord about this, that it should leave me. But he said to me, 'My grace is sufficient for you, for my power is made perfect in weakness.' Therefore I will boast all the more gladly of my weaknesses, so that the power of Christ may rest upon me" (2 Corinthians 12:8–9).

Jesus set a high standard with His command to bring the little children to Him, regardless of diagnosis. Children's ministry volunteers can more easily obey Christ's command and follow His example when they interact with kids in the context of their strengths and their needs, and when they are equipped. Our prayer is that this book will help equip you for the task. So let's learn how to use this book to accommodate the needs of all the children who come to your church to meet Jesus.

How to Use This Book

Company's coming!
These two words can evoke a variety of emotions.

- Joy
- Panic
- Irritation
- Excitement

Whatever our emotions when company's coming, we as hosts must spring into action. We have tables to set, grocery lists to make and powder rooms to scrub. And, whether we're serving pizza on paper plates or lobster on our best china, we have planning to do. Even the most inveterate hosts among us agree that when we can pause, pour a cup of coffee, and plan purposefully, our dinner parties are more enjoyable for everyone. Think of *Every Child Welcome* as your guide, written to assist in your purposeful planning in a variety of ways.

As a Planning Tool: Planning for children's ministry programs is not much different from planning for a dinner party. We want our guests to feel welcome and nurtured, enjoy each other's company, and be enriched and nourished by the conversation. Moreover, we want them to leave feeling content and excited to return. When our guests have special needs, we must consider this in our preparation. Just as we create a menu to accommodate dietary restrictions, we must be sure that our children's ministry activities accommodate the unique needs of the children in our care. In doing so, we increase the likelihood that they'll digest the important concepts we're presenting. We want the hour we spend with them to increase their knowledge and nourish their souls.

As a Cookbook: Like a good cook who turns to a favorite selection of recipes to accommodate every guest who's coming to dinner, you can use this book to accommodate the children you work with. It provides a menu of helpful tips, activities, and information. As you get to know your students, you can choose activities that will enhance their learning, meet their needs and hold their attention.

As a Menu of Options: Do you want to create a welcoming environment before kids arrive? Then turn to chapter 1, *Setting the Table.* You'll find ideas about how to welcome children and set a positive tone in chapter 2, *Greeting the Guests.* Chapter 3 provides appetizers so kids can learn more effectively by connecting new information to what they already know. Chapter 4 explains how to create a positive environment so every child feels welcome. We have included main-dish strategies for reinforcing the main idea of a lesson, building background knowledge and reviewing important concepts in chapter 5. Chapter 6 provides a selection of side dishes: hands-on activities to supplement instruction and to increase attention and participation. For special days like Christmas, Easter, and Pentecost, turn to chapter 7, *Party Time Treats*, which describes activities to keep those days holy—and wholly understandable—to all kids.

In addition, chapter 8, *Service with a Smile*, is devoted to service activities, because we know that all kids—including those with special needs—can effectively serve the kingdom. We've designed strategies for wrapping up an activity effectively in chapter 9, *Washing Up*, and for providing reinforcement for continued learning at home in chapter 10, *To-Go Box.* Finally, because even the best cooks and children's ministry workers can get stuck in a rut, you'll find a menu of books, blogs, and websites in the resource section at the back of the book, so that you can supplement your understanding of disabilities, special needs, and best practices.

We hope this book will become just like that well-worn cookbook on your kitchen shelf, with dog-eared pages and your own notes scrawled in the margins. We also hope the children you are working with will learn some of these recipes by heart, so they can taste and see that the Lord is good!

Chapter 1

Setting the Table: Creating a Welcoming Space for Children

We've all experienced that awkward moment at a dinner party. We've gone through the buffet line and aren't quite sure where we're supposed to go next. We stand, uncertain between the dining and living rooms wondering what to do. Sit down and begin eating? Or wait until everyone has been served? Will we pray together first, or is this a mingling party where we'll stand around and eat? It can be distressing to even the most socially savvy party-goer. The bottom line is that we want our host and hostess to give us clear directions on what to do and where to go.

Planning for children's ministry activities is not much different from planning for a dinner party. We want our guests to feel welcome, enjoy each other's company, and be strengthened by our time together. Most of all, we want them to be excited to return.

Fortunately, we know more than we have ever known about how children learn and we understand their behavior much more intricately. This allows us to plan more proactively for our classes, worship services, and youth groups. However, before we even open our resource books or leader's manuals, we can plan for successful learning.

A Prayer of Preparation

*Lord, as I open the leader's guides to plan for this week,
I am aware of this wonderful opportunity to teach about
You. I ask for Your guidance as I approach this task. You
are a God of order. You created time and space and information. Help me to create a sense of order for these children
so that nothing will distract them from learning about You.*

Strategy 1—Creating a Team

As with most ministries, special needs inclusion works best when a cohesive team is in place. After all, we're the body of Christ, and we need the gifts of everyone to be a complete community. We only need to look to the longstanding public school method of identifying and educating kids with disabilities to know that a team approach works. Here are some tips for creating your team:

- *Identify stakeholders from all areas of your church.* This includes facilities, children's ministry, leadership (elder board or pastor), parents of kids with special needs, parents of typically develop-ing kids, medical or educational professionals from the church or community.
- *Invite anyone who might be interested.* Remember, this is a min-istry of *inclusion.* Begin your ministry with a culture of accep-tance and model that everyone who has a willing heart has gifts that can and should be used.
- *Find another church with a similar ministry.* There is no need to reinvent the wheel. Invite the advice and counsel of other lead-ers, especially those who are connected in your community.

Strategy 2—Web-Based Communication Tools

When it comes to communication, our world moves faster than ever before. Gone are the days of telegrams and carbon copies. Technol-ogy can definitely enhance our ministry to those with disabilities. Con-sider the following online tools to see what might work for your team.

- *Ning.* Mike Woods, Director of Special Needs Friends Ministry at First Baptist Orlando, uses Ning with his ministry volunteers. He says, "It's a social networking site that, for our ministry page, is 'invite-only.' We can talk, share information, post training videos, and keep it only to members who are invited." (www.ning.com)

- *Google+.* Another way to create online group communication. (www.plus.google.com)
- *Facebook.* This social media site has an option for closed groups which might be helpful for general communication between parents, volunteers, and Sunday school staff. Uses include posting Bible memory verses, links to curriculum activities or videos, and outlines of plans or upcoming events. (www.facebook.com)
- *Free Conference Call.* This recommendation also comes from Mike Woods: "We've been able to have volunteer or buddy meetings from the convenience of everyone's home." (www.freeconferencecall.com)
- *Yammer.* Laura Haas, who works in Children's and Inclusion Ministry at Faith Family Church in Canton, Ohio, recommended this resource. (www.yammer.com)
- *Wiggio.* Our friend and colleague Sara Moses suggested this tool. She used it for several groups, including an inclusion ministry. (www.wiggio.com)
- *Live Binders.* This resource was recommended by Michelle Thomas-Bush, Associate Pastor for Youth and Their Families at Myers Park Presbyterian Church in Charlotte, North Carolina. It allows you to upload docs, slide shows, links, forms, and other information to share with your team. (www.livebinders.com)
- *Google Docs.* This is another method of sharing information, including training materials, spread sheets, presentations, even brainstorming lists. Google also has a calendar feature that team members can access and edit. (docs.google.com)

Remember, you can use these tools for a variety of different reasons. One web-based tool need not fit all of your needs. As you peruse these sites, keep in mind that **privacy is paramount**.

In your ministry, you'll be privy to sensitive information about children and their families. As such, you cannot rely solely on the privacy capabilities of social media sites. **Your volunteer and staff training must include in-depth discussions about handling information**.

When training volunteers, include a rule that forbids sharing ministry site passwords with friends, family, or colleagues who are not directly involved in the ministry. Privacy settings are only as sensitive as the people who are using them.

One final note: God created people long before computers ever appeared on the scene. So put people first. There isn't a high-speed connection anywhere that can ever replace human relationships. While technology, used well and wisely, can enhance communication, it won't ever replace community.

Strategy 3—Policies and Procedures: Create Them from the Inside Out

Katie filed into the conference room, along with other new hires at the psychiatric hospital. This was her first job, and she was excited to get started. She would be teaching in the acute-care classroom, as well as helping to design a new unit for young children. She and her new colleagues looked around anxiously and made polite small talk in hushed tones. The director of human resources finally entered the room.

The chit-chat ended as he launched into a litany of policies and procedures. The new hires watched a video that featured pretty, tanned actors portraying staff and patients. Scenes in the video showed laughing families, therapists and patients engaged in meaningful dialogue, and a staff-patient volleyball game, complete with laughter and applause.

Katie couldn't wait to get started. However, during the time she worked there, she experienced nothing remotely similar to the lovely infomercial. Later, she realized that the hospital was very high on external policies and procedures. Employees were told what to wear, how to speak, what to say in public about the hospital. It was rather like biting into a mouth-watering, chocolate frosted, cream-filled donut, only to discover sour jelly inside.

What does this have to do with starting a special needs ministry? Simple: Your policies and procedures must be developed from the in-

Sample Special Needs Ministry Mission Statement

Our Special Needs Ministry has a two-fold mission:

1. To help our church become a place where children with special needs and their families are welcomed and included as full participants in the life of the church.

2. To help children with special needs know, love, and share the Lord.

side out. Too often, we belabor the formation of policies, and become mired in the minutiae. We need to avoid this in order to formulate policies and procedures that will make sense. We can do this by identifying the heart of the ministry: its mission.

With your team assembled, discuss the mission of your ministry. It's rather like choosing your destination for a trip. Until you do this, it's impractical and frustrating to pack up the car and drive. It will be important to review your church's mission statement, as well as the mission statements of the church's ministries for children and youth. Savvy special needs ministry planners will also consider the mission statement for the adult education ministry, knowing that kids with special needs will transition to adulthood one day.

Strategy 4—Security Issues: How to Keep Safety First

Safety first! This motto used by Scout troops applies to ministry environments as well. Safety is an ideal that must be actively pursued, and consistently monitored, particularly when working with children who have special needs. Several aspects of ministry require safety inspections as well as careful planning.

Policies for Staff and Volunteers

All volunteers and staff must have a criminal background check prior to working with children. Although you've known Mrs. Ellis for decades and are sure she would never, ever harm anyone, you must show wisdom in staffing programs. Often, local police departments will help with the screening process, or churches can use a service like www.protectmyministry.com to obtain information.

In addition to a background check, volunteers should be trained to effectively and safely manage emergencies. If a child has a seizure or an allergic reaction, volunteers and staff will need to know how to care for the child and keep him/her safe until help arrives. By implementing training and even practicing procedures periodically, adults gain skills to anticipate and manage crises.

Finally, no child should ever be alone with an adult. The gold standard for safety in this area would be two supervisory adults who are not married to one another. Many couples enjoy teaching together, and this can be a very effective ministry for a marriage. If this is the case, be certain that the couple is not alone with an individual student. This protects both the child and the volunteers.

Facilities

Not all church buildings are accessible to those with physical disabilities. However, all buildings can be made safe. When planning for a program or class, be certain to assess the space for safety. The checklist below can help:

- Are outlets covered?
- Is the furniture in good condition? Can it collapse or fall over with normal use?
- Can you see every child in the room with the current arrangement?
- Is there a window to the hallway in each classroom door?
- Do windows/doors to the outside lock so that children cannot escape?
- Are scissors or other sharp objects placed away from kids' reach?
- Is there a bathroom or sink in the classroom? If so, how will this be monitored to prevent injury?

Staffing for Safety

Sometimes, the best way to provide security is by recruiting some extra volunteers. Safety patrol volunteers can be stationed at exit doors to be certain that kids don't leave the building. In addition, these folks can be assigned as rovers who move from class to class to provide additional behavioral support when necessary.

In addition to the safety patrol, consider policies and procedures for bathroom breaks and diapering. Each church handles this differently; some churches page parents for diaper duty while others have a diapering station in the nursery. When considering the needs of older children with disabilities, be sensitive to their emotional development as well as their physical needs. Creating a diapering station in an adult bathroom that is behind a partition can be one respectful way to manage this. A private room for this purpose can also be an alternative, though it is usually difficult to designate a room for this because of the demands for space. Whatever policy is adopted, remember that when volunteers or staff are changing diapers, they should not be alone with a child. This is a time when two adults, not married to each other, should be working together.

Safety procedures can be tedious and even uncomfortable to discuss. However, they set a tone of professionalism, care, and respect to which parents—and kids—will respond.

Strategy 5—Space and Materials Planning

Before a dinner party, we sometimes need to pay close attention to seating arrangements. For example, we know that Cousin Jeffrey likes to be seated on the end of the table; he's a lefty who doesn't want to bump elbows throughout the meal. And of course, we don't want Aunt Sally and Grandpa seated near each other. Remember last Thanksgiving when they had that debate about foreign policy? Aunt Sally locked herself in the powder room for forty-five minutes after that showdown. We also like to arrange our pre-dinner space so that guests know how to find drinks, appetizers, and comfortable seating—out of the way of the cook's last-minute preparations.

Set-Up

Similarly, when we plan for activities, we want the space to reflect our desire for children's comfort and learning. When kids enter, they should feel welcome and comfortable. Clearly defined areas with distinct purposes help kids know what to do and how to behave when they enter the room.

In addition, if you are planning special activities—for example a stage to act out a story, or a cave to help kids experience the empty tomb on Easter morning—the set-up should be done in advance. The most enriching activity can be ruined if kids lose attention while leaders assemble the activity. Finally, we know that seating arrangements can make a difference. Knowing how to group children in the available space can assist them with focus, cooperation, and learning.

Materials

Make a list of all the props, papers, art supplies, and books you will need for your activity. This might seem tedious, but consider our dinner party analogy: Everything runs much more smoothly when your ingredients, dishes, and place cards are at the ready. It's awful when the host of the party needs to run to the attic to retrieve a serving dish. By making a list and setting the table for participants, you ensure that everything needed is at your fingertips.

Strategy 6—Schedule and Transition Planning

An education mentor shared this bit of wisdom: "You have to plan every single minute. Kids get in trouble when they don't know what they're supposed to be doing."

We don't want kids to get into trouble, especially when we can prevent it. Thorough planning can eliminate many worries. To see how that happens, let's compare two activity plans for a second grade midweek program.

Plan One:

- Kids arrive, do worksheet
- Opening activity (procedure in leader's manual)
- Read Bible story
- Have kids write in their journals
- Talk about field trip to the nursing home (next week's activity)
- Work on group mural
- Discuss the importance of obeying God
- Clean up the room
- Sing closing song

Plan Two:

7:00-7:05	Kids arrive, write on Weekly News Board, work on tabletop activities
7:05-7:06	Transition to front of the room by playing Follow the Leader
7:06-7:10	Introduce the evening's topic, have kids pick color cubes from basket; break into small groups according to color to do opening activity (See leader's manual for activity)
7:10-7:20	Read the Bible story from manual; have kids write three facts in their journal. Stand and play Praise Ball (kids tell the group something they're thankful for when they catch the ball)
7:20-7:28	Return to seats while singing "This Little Light of Mine." In preparation for next week's service project (visiting the nursing home), practice introducing each other and asking getting-to-know-you questions.
7:28-7:30	Give verbal and visual directions for group activities. Transition to small group activity rotations (15 minutes each)

- Small group discussion with leader (questions in manual)
- Mural project with teen helper

- Free choice from the back table supervised by teen helper

8:15-8:20 Clean up, closing ceremonies

8:20-? *Veggie Tales* movie until parents arrive

Do you see the difference between the two plans? The first is an outline of activities that shows what thorough planning looks like. The second pays close attention to the situations where kids with special needs are most at risk: arrivals, transitions, and free choice.

The second plan seems tedious. But it works because planning arrivals, transitions, and breaks is just as important as planning your content. You need to plan out these procedures for your group so that everyone is on-task, engaged, and learning. This helps kids learn kindness, turn-taking, and respect. It helps them to function like a church family.

Strategy 7—Creating Quiet Zones: We All Need a Break Now and Then

Children's ministry activities can be crowded, noisy, confusing, and downright overwhelming for kids. More so for children who are sensory sensitive or unable to communicate their feelings effectively. A quiet zone or break zone gives these kids a place where they can calm down and regain a sense of security before rejoining the group.

How To Create a Quiet Zone

By thinking creatively and proactively, quiet zones can be incorporated into most children's ministry activities.

- A corner of a classroom can be fitted out with a portable screen to reduce visual clutter, a bean bag chair, some stress balls, and other soothing items.
- If space allows, a small classroom can be designated as the quiet zone. It can be available during noisy, large group activities such as Awana game time, youth group gatherings, or Sunday morning contemporary worship services. A small church in Wisconsin did this and stocked it with two gym mats, a mirror, chalk, markers, a weighted vest, therapy balls, and a mini-trampoline purchased using funds from a grant received from their denomination. Members of the congregation donated homemade afghans, a boom box, and a small pup tent.

- If you're taking children to someone's house, talk to the host beforehand about creating a quiet zone somewhere. You may want to ask parents to help stock the quiet zone: a cuddly toy, a blanket, or even an iPod for a child who responds well to relaxing music.
- For outdoor excursions, designate a particular place—perhaps a picnic table, a visible area a short distance from the main action, a shelter house, or even a section of the church bus—as the break zone. Stock a backpack with some of the more portable items mentioned above and place it in the quiet zone.

How to Introduce a Quiet Zone

Once the designated quiet zone is ready for use, train volunteers and children so they know how and when to use it. Explain its purpose to volunteers. Go over safety procedures and discuss how to monitor children. Allow kids an opportunity to try out the zone and become comfortable with both what the space is like and when to use it. This can be done during a get-acquainted tour with the child and parents (see Strategy 10—*Welcome Aboard! Planning a Church Visit for Children with Disabilities*, page 25), or during one of the first times a child attends the program.

For many kids, knowing a quiet zone is available eases their anxieties, and they won't need to use it. For others, the quiet zone allows them to participate in some activities they might otherwise avoid. The quiet zone speaks volumes to parents, too. Its presence tells them their children are valued enough to make them feel safe. Parents who hear that message are more likely to make the effort, bring their children to church, and encourage them to stay.

Strategy 8—Rooms that Make Scents

What happens when you walk past a bakery and inhale the aroma of fresh bread? You suddenly feel hungry. How about when you walk past a Christmas tree lot on a frosty morning and the smell of pine and cold fills your nostrils? Does it make you want to sing Christmas carols?

If ordinary scents and aromas can affect adults that powerfully, imagine what they do to children with sensory sensitivities and allergies. Kids on the autism spectrum are prone to sensory sensitivity to smells, also known as olfactory sensitivity, but sensory sensitivity also affects children with other special needs. Several simple modifications can be made before kids walk through the doors to make the classroom space welcoming to sensory-sensitive kids and safer for those with allergies.

Educate and Advocate

Start by educating others in your church about sensory sensitivities and how they affect kids. Advocate for a children's ministry fragrance-free policy. Pass out notes at registration describing the policy. Ask the custodians to use scent-free cleaning products, scent-free soap, and paper products in the bathrooms. Remove air fresheners from the premises: free-standing, plug-ins, and aerosols. Also, ask others to refrain from using candles or incense.

Adjust Your Location

Ask for a classroom as far away from the bathrooms or kitchen as possible. Inside your classroom, use creative seating arrangements. Seat children with sensory sensitivities near a window so they can get fresh air. Seat them as far away from classroom aromas (craft table, snacks, children with body odor) as possible.

Adjust Your Hygiene Habits

Use scent-free toiletry products and refrain from wearing perfume, cologne, and aftershave lotion. Ask any volunteers working with you to do so, too. A classroom that accommodates for kids with sensory sensitivities encourages them to attend more frequently and makes participation much more pleasant for them. Any way you sniff it, it just makes *scents*!

How kids with olfactory sensitivity respond to scents:

- Fixate on a smell because it is overpowering
- Nausea
- Smell foods before eating and smell materials before using them
- Recognize smells before others

How kids with allergies respond to scents:

- Headaches
- Wheezing or difficulty breathing
- Runny or stuffy nose
- Sneezing
- Skin rash

Strategy 9—Other Sensory Issues

Worship leaders everywhere have heard it all before.

- The music is too loud!
- The music is too soft!
- Why do we need all these video screens?
- Can't we use more video?
- The lights during the sermon aren't bright enough!
- I can't concentrate on the pastor with all of the lights on in the sanctuary.
- Why are we using these chairs? The pews were much cozier.
- Can't we go back to using chairs? They're more comfortable than these pews.

It's impossible to keep everyone happy. We all have preferences about our church environment. From music to lighting to seating and volume, we know what we like. For some kids, however, these sensory components go beyond personal preference. Children with sensory integration disorder or sensory sensitivities can become anxious, afraid, or unbearably uncomfortable when the environmental input overwhelms them. While we can't predict or meet the needs of every individual, we can set up our rooms and programs to create a sensory-friendly experience.

Sound
Rather than having loud music playing when kids arrive, choose quieter, slower music. This will be easier for kids who are sensitive to sound, and even typically developing kids will respond to the more relaxed tone you're setting. In addition, use chimes or a train whistle as a signal for attention. Loud noises, such as clanging bells, buzzers, and even voices, can be difficult for kids with auditory sensitivities. During singing time, allow kids who have a sensitivity to noise to stand in the hallway; they can still see and hear the worship music, but the noise will be more manageable. For children with more pronounced sensitivities, consider offering noise-canceling headphones.

Visuals
We do love to decorate our classrooms. Bulletin boards, kids' artwork, and murals make the space welcoming and attractive. To avoid having too much of a good thing, implement some of these tips.

- As you decorate, leave some uncluttered space for the eyes to rest.
- Put out just a few decorations at a time and rotate in new ones when the previous ones come down. This can make the room more visually appealing to all kids, and communicate a sense of organization.
- Choose neutral or muted tones if you have the opportunity to choose colors for a new space. While bright colors are fun, they can be overwhelming . Allow color to come in on posters or bulletin boards.
- Consider lighting choices carefully. Fluorescent lights are inexpensive and widely available, but they are also overwhelming for kids with sensory sensitivities. Incandescent bulbs are preferable. If you have fluorescents in your current space, remove some of the bulbs to reduce the glare. You can also purchase filters or materials to make light-softening filters at www.educationalinsights.com.

Textures

Children with sensory processing disorders often struggle to feel comfortable with certain textures. As a result, parents of kids with these issues embrace tag-free clothing, as the feel of a tag can be irritating or painful for their child. To offer "tag-free" comfort at church, try these strategies.

- Provide comfortable places for kids to sit. Bean bag chairs and rockers can offer a soft place to land.
- Offer choices during activities that involve textures. For example, a child might choose to color with markers rather than finger paint.
- Allow children to refuse snacks or bring their own; eating involves textures, too.

When we consider these sensory issues, we can set kids up for a more relaxed and comfortable time in church—a place where we want everyone to be comfortable.

Strategy 10—Welcome Aboard! Planning a Church Visit for Children with Disabilities

For children with disabilities, new experiences (such as coming to church) require some extra planning. Often, when a student with special needs visits a new place or experiences a change in routine, he or she experiences anxiety. This can set the child (and teachers and classmates) up for failure …and his parents for isolation and disappointment. Offering an opportunity to practice new routines and experience unfamiliar settings can greatly increase the likelihood for success.

Consider, for example, an experience recently created at the Philadelphia International Airport for families affected by autism. Families come to the airport, check in, go through security and board their plane. Dr. Wendy Ross, who designed the program, described the economic impact of difficult travel: "These families [affected by autism] are not going out…. So for businesses, that's a huge loss." Dr. Ross also mentioned that the goal of the program is to educate both airline officials and families, giving them strategies "to build a bridge between them."[1]

When families affected by autism don't buy airline tickets, purchase goods and services, or book hotel rooms, it certainly does affect the economy. When they don't come to church, it affects the body of Christ. We're incomplete.

Build a Bridge

In order to build a bridge, we can provide an opportunity for children with autism, sensory issues, or other behavioral special needs to *practice* coming to children's programs, thus allowing them to become familiar with the building and routines. This simulation should take place on a day or evening when the building is relatively quiet. The experience might include the following:

- Checking in at the information/name tag table
- Entering the classroom or activity space
- Reading the schedule for the activity
- Listening to music
- Looking at pictures of other children in the program
- Working on a small craft or coloring sheet
- Taking a bathroom break (if the child needs assistance, two adults or a parent should be present)
- Praying together
- Enjoying a snack
- Reading a Bible story
- Saying goodbye and leaving the building

---

1. http://www.abc-7.com/story/13938553/program-helps-autistic-kids-handle-airlin es?clienttype=generic&mobilecgbypass, accessed February 3, 2014.

Build a Short Bridge

All of this can be accomplished in twenty to thirty minutes. Although this investment of time is a sacrifice, it will likely pay huge dividends for everyone, as the child will be better prepared to attend children's ministry programs. In addition, the child may begin to recognize the children's ministry wing as a supportive, safe place. The parents will hopefully enjoy the luxury of an easier drop-off time, along with the ability to blend in and perhaps even sip a cup of coffee before attending adult church activities.

Bridge Building Safety Tips

Tip 1: Before sharing photos of other children, obtain signed photo releases from parents.

Tip 2: Always have two adults or a parent present when assisting children in the bathroom.

Strategy 11—Proactive Communication with Parents

Every child is unique, and so is every parent. Thus, parents' communication styles and expectations may vary widely. Some parents might come to you with more information than you think you need. Others will drop off their child without a word, just a weary look of relief. A few might even show up on Sunday morning, and with palpable frustration say, "Here, you deal with him for a while."

Special Needs Ministry Covenant

Research about parent-teacher relationships indicates that shared expectations lead to more positive, collaborative problem-solving and higher rates of learning for children. That's why it's important for us to communicate clearly about our plans for kids' programming, rules for behavior, and also our own need for information. One way to do this is by providing a covenant like the Special Needs Ministry Covenant, which can be found in Appendix A (page 165). It clearly lists the rights and responsibilities of every member of the ministry team, including the child.

Letter of Introduction

In addition to an agreement like this, you can communicate proactively in more general ways. For example, send a letter of introduction prior to the program year. In this letter, invite parents to call or email you if they'd like to share information about their children. In this letter, also indicate that you are very interested in learning about each child's strengths, as well as any special needs they might have. This underscores your awareness of special needs issues, as well as your willingness to learn about each child.

Classroom News

While individual conversations provide valuable information to volunteers, parents will often benefit from general classroom news as well. Create a private Facebook page or publish a newsletter to inform parents of upcoming events and provide ideas for reinforcing lessons at home.

Positive, proactive communication takes planning and patience. However, this investment of time will likely pay great dividends in relationships which ultimately benefit the kingdom.

Strategy 12—Extra, Extra, Read All About It

Have you ever counted the number of people your students and their families meet between the front door of the church and your classroom? The number may be surprising, even overwhelming. It may make you wonder how to make all those people part of an unofficial and effective church welcoming team. The weekly bulletin and church newsletter can be a good place to begin. Here are a few ways to use these familiar tools to promote special needs ministries and educate your entire church family:

- Ask the person who creates the weekly church bulletin and/or monthly newsletter to include a special needs ministry announcement in every issue. The sidebar has several examples.

Special Needs Ministry Announcements

Sample One: The members of _____ Church welcome people who live with disabilities. Please ask a greeter, usher, or the welcome booth host if you need any assistance. You can also call the church office to discuss your needs or send an email using the contact information on the front of the bulletin.

Sample Two: Our church is committed to fulfilling Jesus' command in Matthew 19:14 to let the children come to him. We welcome children with special needs to worship with us and attend children's ministry activities. To learn more, contact _____ _____ by phone (000-000-0000) or email (childrensministry@yourchurch.com).

- Write a short "Did you know?" special needs filler for the monthly newsletter. See the sidebar for examples.
- Offer to pen a special needs column for the newsletter. If once a month is too much, how about once or twice a year?
- Once you've taken advantage of paper-and-ink options, move on to electronic options young parents love. If your church has a website, ask the webmaster to add any of the above to it. Ditto for the children's ministry page on the website and the church Facebook page.

By using both hard copy and electronic options, you can deliver two powerful messages to two important groups. You increase special needs sensitivity and education within the general congregation. And you let families of kids with special needs know they are valued and welcome members of the body of Christ. Now that's a special needs win-win situation for sure.

Monthly Newsletter Special Needs Filler Samples

- *Did you know* some children with special needs are sensory sensitive? They perceive sounds, smells, lights, textures, and flavors very intensely and may be scared or repulsed by them.
- *Did you know* some children are highly sensitive to sound? They may wear headphones during worship to make participation more comfortable.
- *Did you know* some people with special needs in our church can't control their emotions or speech? When they speak or shout during worship, know that the joyful noises they make are sweet to God's ears.
- *Did you know* that many children at _____ Church live with food allergies? That's why our nursery and children's ministry programs offer allergy-free food options for kids allergic to nuts, eggs, dairy products, soy, and corn.
- *Did you know* that _____ _____ leads our special needs ministry? Please call her at 000-000-0000 for more information about how we serve children with special needs.

Strategy 13—Book Talk: Beefing Up the Special Needs Section of Your Church Library

During Jolene's years as an elementary teacher, she welcomed students with a variety of special needs into her mainstream classroom. She often read carefully selected children's books to her students to demystify special needs and encourage children to be patient and compassionate with one another. You can accomplish the same goal by beefing up your church library's selection of special needs-related books. Begin with children's books, but if possible, also add books of interest to adults who want to learn about special needs and books that offer support to special needs families.

Start by contacting the person in charge of ordering books for your church library to explain your goals. Offer to prepare a book wish list to be used when ordering new books. If you get the okay, here's a good book list to get you started:

For Younger Children
Just the Way I Am: God's Good Design in Disability; Krista Horning (Christian Focus Publications, 2011)
In Jesse's Shoes: Appreciating Kids with Special Needs; Beverly Lewis (Bethany House, 2007)
A Friend Like Simon; Kate Gaynor (Special Stories Publishing, 2009): Autism Spectrum Disorder
My Friend Isabelle; Eliza Woloson (Woodbine House, 2003): Down Syndrome
Ellie Bean the Drama Queen; A Children's Book About Sensory Processing Disorder; Jennie Harding (Sensory World, 2011)
Thank You, Mr. Falker; Patricia Polacco (Philomel, 2012): Dyslexia

For Older Children
Window Boy; Andrea White (Bright Sky Press, 2008): Cerebral Palsy
Small Steps: The Year I Got Polio; Peg Kehret (Albert Whitman & Co., 1996)

No Library at Your Church?

Go to your public library, research their special needs offerings, and present the public librarian with your wish list. Ask the person in charge of the newsletter at your church to feature a special needs book from the public library each month.

For Adults

Same Lake, Different Boat: Coming Alongside People Touched by Disability; Stephanie Hubach (P & R Publishing, 2006)

A Different Dream for My Child: Meditations for Parents of Critically or Chronically Ill Children; Jolene Philo (Discovery House Publishers, 2009)

Different Dream Parenting: A Practical Guide to Raising a Child with Special Needs; Jolene Philo (Discovery House Publishers, 2011)

Uncommon Beauty: Crisis Parenting from Day One; Margaret Meder (Beaver's Pond Press, 2012)

The Church and Disability: The Weblog Disabled Christianity; Jeff McNair (CreateSpace, 2010)

A Good and Perfect Gift: Faith, Expectations, and a Little Girl Named Penny; Amy Julia Becker (Bethany House, 2011)

5 Tips to Stretch the Church Library Budget

1. Does your denomination have a church bookstore? They may offer discounts and coupons to church libraries.

2. Contact publishers and offer to review special needs books for your church newsletter or personal blog. The publishers will send free copies which you can donate to your church library once you've completed the review.

3. Check the book orders kids bring home from school. They offer great deals.

4. Check Amazon and eBay frequently.

5. Publish your book wish list in the church bulletin and newsletter, and include it on the church's website. Ask people to donate books from the list.

Chapter 2

Greeting Your Guests: Communicating Warmth and Safety at Arrival Time

Have you ever been invited to a dinner party where you didn't know anyone well? Did you stand on the doorstep, take a deep breath, and ring the bell with a trembling finger? Then you know how parents and their children feel when they visit a church for the first time. The trembly feeling is often double strength for parents bringing a child with special needs, as thoughts race through their minds: Will my child be welcomed? Will my daughter be valued? Will she find a friend? Will someone care enough to learn my son's name? Will the environment make my child feel safe?

This chapter is all about making a good first impression, so that the fears of parents and their children are quickly dispelled. The strategies you're about to learn can help you—and everyone else in your church family—make a good impression in the parking lot, the lobby, the registration table, in the hallways of the children's ministry wing, and finally, when a child new to your children's ministry program enters your meeting space.

A Prayer for Welcoming Children to Children's Ministry Programs

*Lord, right now it's quiet in this place. Soon, though,
I'll hear footsteps running down the hall and murmurs
between parents and kids. Children will cross the threshold,
and I will have one hour to teach—and reach them. Help
me to welcome them warmly, Lord, so their hearts will be
ready to learn about You.*

Strategy 1—Create a Gentle Entrance

We all know that moment. The magical moment when we enter a room, turn on the lights and then suddenly, without warning—*Surprise!* Our friends jump out, clapping, laughing, and racing to embrace us, all in the good fun of celebration. Once we catch our breath, we're usually quite pleased.

For many children with sensory difficulties or anxiety, our well-intentioned greetings are rather like an unexpected and unwelcome surprise party. In our efforts to make every moment of church fun and exciting, our entryways sometimes mimic carnival spaces with loud music, murals, and decorative lights. While this sets the mood for many typically developing kids, those with special needs might find this welcome quite unwelcoming. Fortunately, we can remedy this quite easily by creating a gentle entrance. Here's how:

- *Designate one door* into the church as a gentle entrance.
- *Create a sign* that informs parents of this entrance. It can say: If you or your child prefer a quiet start to church, please enter through our gentle entrance on the _____.
- *Train greeters* who staff this entrance to use quiet voices and refrain from hugs or high fives that are overwhelming or even painful for some children.
- *Turn down lights to low.* If using fluorescent lighting, remove some of the bulbs to soften the lighting.
- *Play nature sounds,* quiet instrumental music, or turn off music altogether in this entrance.

A quiet entrance will pay huge dividends for families. It's the kind of gentle welcome that can create a worshipful Sunday morning for the whole family.

Strategy 2—What's in a Name:
Why Greeting Kids by Name Makes a Difference

Picture this—a busy church hallway, full of exuberant children. As is often the case at children's ministry programs, the pace between activities is quick. Nevertheless, the volunteer leader remains placid. She checks in with her volunteers, prepares for her duties, and communicates with other staff. None of this interferes with the most important task: greeting the children. She greets every single child by name:

Good morning, Michael!
It's great to see you today, Tiara!
I'm so glad you're here, Kieran!

Every greeting—just like every child—is unique.

Why Using a Child's Name Is Important

A classroom management philosophy called "Responsive Classroom" emphasizes the importance of knowing children—and greeting them—by name. One administrator reflected, "By the end of morning meeting, every single child has heard his or her name spoken aloud. That sends a powerful message that each individual matters to the group."

What Using a Child's Name Says

Clearly, the leader described above understands this. She is modeling several things to children and the volunteers working with her:

- She knows the children in her care.
- She cares about them as individuals.
- She cares about their learning.

In addition, she is modeling something even greater for the children in her program. In John 10:2–3, we hear Jesus say,

> But he who enters by the door is the shepherd of the sheep. To him the gatekeeper opens. The sheep hear his voice, and he calls his own sheep by name and leads them out.

By using children's names, the children's ministry leader models Jesus' love for them. Because, like her, Jesus knows our names!

Strategy 3—Check-In and Name Tag Know-How

Names are one of the most powerful tools available to adults working with children. By making name tags an integral part of the check-in process, we accomplish two tasks at once: gathering information about those in attendance and distributing name tags. The name tags can also be used to alert all volunteers about the individual behavioral issues and safety concerns for each child, while ensuring confidentiality and promoting consistency.

How to Create a Check-In System

The development of an effective check-in and name tag system requires some planning and collaboration ahead of time. Consider meeting with other teachers and the program coordinator so you can brainstorm together. These questions can help you create a name tag protocol that will function for months and even years to come:

- How can we design one, consistent check in system to be used by typically developing children and those with special needs in a variety of children's ministry programs?
- Should our children's ministry invest in a computerized check-in/checkout program or can we manage without it?
- What codes or symbols can be added to the name tags to alert all volunteers of potential safety risks concerning children who are potential runners, have food allergies, special bathroom needs, seizures, or other safety issues?
- How can the check-in process and name tags be used to ensure children are released to the designated parent, guardian, or adult?
- How can the system help reach parents in case of an emergency?
- How will volunteers be educated concerning the check-in process and name tag system?

How to Create a Simple Name Tag System

Choosing the simplest answer to those questions is key to creating an uncomplicated name tag system. Here are some ideas to help you accomplish that goal:

- Create a central check-in station where volunteers sign in all children and issue name tags. That way teachers and leaders can concentrate on completing activities with kids.

- Use the same kind of name tag for all children. Choose tags big enough for a child's name and any codes or visual cues necessary for children with special needs.
- Order colored wristbands or add colored sticker dots (from an office supply or discount store) as safety alerts: blue for food allergies, red for kids who run, green for special bathroom needs, and so on. If your church uses a computerized name tag system, printed symbols can be added to the tag instead.
- Add a wristband for circumstances not addressed by the normal system. Special needs ministry expert Denise Briley uses wristbands to alert volunteers that a child may be prone to running and may try to leave the building. This strategy provides communication without stigmatizing the child.
- Ask parents to sign in at the check-in station and sign out when their children are released. Or put a number on each name tag and give parents an ID tag with the same number. They can present the ID tag to the ministry worker, who will check it against the name tag before a child is released.

When Your Children's Ministry Goes on the Road

Try these ideas when the situation demands more than wristbands and name tags:

- **T-shirts.** These can be a helpful identification tool for retreats and outreach events. Children can be quickly identified when they're wearing the same brightly colored shirts. T-shirts can also be a helpful way to keep small groups and leaders together. Assign each grade level or small group a certain color shirt to make it easy to find a leader and peers.
- **USB bracelets.** Leaders need quick access to emergency medical information when traveling to church camp or on mission trips. One convenient way to manage this is by loading information onto a USB drive that attaches to a bracelet. The information remains with the child, eliminating the need to find a file or safety card. Information on these drives should be shared only with parental permission, only when absolutely necessary, and in strict confidence.

- Ask parents to list a cell phone number and indicate where they will be in the building, and where they sit during worship, in case of an emergency.
- Provide training for new volunteers and communicate changes as they occur, or annually.

Once you have a check-in system in place and volunteers know how to use it, it will become an integral part of your children's ministry. But like any tool, it needs regular maintenance to function best. Once a year, ask parents and volunteers for input about what they like and for ways to improve the system. If changes are made, educate everyone so the power of each child's name can be used to keep them safe and to communicate the care and compassion of Christ.

Strategy 4—Peer Greeters: Helping Children Welcome Each Other

Often, children with special needs struggle socially. Making and keeping friends at school and in the neighborhood is incredibly difficult. We can increase the likelihood that kids with disabilities will find friends at children's ministry activities by training their typically developing peers.

How to Recruit Peer Greeters

One way to accomplish this is to recruit peer greeters. How can this be done?

- Observe children who attend children's ministry events frequently. Those who demonstrate a calm demeanor, the ability to follow directions, and an accepting, understanding spirit make excellent candidates for this role.
- Once potential peer greeters have been identified, talk with their parent or guardian to be sure that they may volunteer in this capacity. Taking on the role of greeter means arriving a bit early, and therefore, requires the chauffeur skills of an adult. In addition, it will be important to discuss the expectations for this role with the parents so they can reinforce these ideas with their child.

How to Train Peer Greeters

Once you've recruited peer greeters, they need training. These tips can help:

- Work with peer greeters to help them understand the importance of their role in welcoming new children.
- Talk about how it feels to be new to Sunday school, club night, VBS, or children's church and how we want to show God's love to all of the children who visit the church.
- Discuss similarities and differences as well, and emphasize that while we all have strengths and difficulties, we're all loved by Jesus.
- Finally, role play with the kids, allowing them to practice welcoming a new child.

By training children to welcome and understand those with disabilities, we not only allow them to serve the church, but we also help them form friendships that can make a lasting impact on the kingdom.

Strategy 5—Schedules: Helping Kids Know What to Expect

Think about what we do each week before we enter the sanctuary: we greet the usher and take our bulletin, which gives us the order of worship, the hymns we'll sing, and other important information. Why? Because we like to know what to expect. So do our kids.

Why to Tell Kids What to Expect

Children with disabilities often have a heightened need to know the schedule ahead of time. This need exists for several reasons:

- Separating from parents can be frightening for children who have anxiety; they will want to know when they will be reunited with Mom or Dad.
- Understanding new rules and procedures can be overwhelming for children who have autism spectrum disorders.
- Children with attention issues benefit from the structure a schedule provides.

How to Tell Kids What to Expect

Therefore, having a routine that involves reviewing the schedule can be a critical component to any children's ministry activity. To accomplish this, simply write out the plans for your time together on a whiteboard or a piece of chart paper. The schedule might look something like this:

Today is Sunday, January 17, 2015
We will write our Weekly News and talk about our week.
We will pray together.
After we pray, we will read our Bible story.
We will go to the big room and sing worship songs.
We will work on a craft.
We will go home.

To help children better understand this schedule, include icons or pictures of each activity. Many children with special needs fare best with these kinds of visuals. When all of the children have arrived, take time to read the schedule together so that everyone knows what to expect. This short routine will enhance your time together because it meets the needs of children who easily become anxious, overwhelmed, or benefit from structure.

Strategy 6—Visual Schedules: The Eyes Have It

Visual schedule is a new name for an idea that's been around for a long time. Visual schedules display the steps of an activity in the order in which they will occur using words, pictures, photographs, icons, and sometimes actual objects. They are effective tools for kids with special needs who respond much better to what they see than what they hear. These kids may not understand verbal instructions or may be unable to recall the steps or correct sequence for multi-step processes. A visual schedule allows them to see the directions, step-by-step and in the proper sequence.

When to Use Visual Schedules

The schedules can be used in a multitude of situations, from listing every activity on Sunday morning to the steps of one specific activity, such as hand-washing in the bathroom or completing a project and cleaning up the craft table. Generally, the length of the visual schedule should increase with a child's chronological or developmental age. Fewer steps, shorter time spans, and more concrete symbols are appropriate for young children and those with developmental levels. More steps, a

**Visual Symbols:
From Concrete to Abstract**

- Actual Objects
- Photographs
- Colored Line Drawings
- Black and White Line Drawings
- Text

broader time span, and more abstract symbols can be used for children who are older or at a higher developmental level.

Components of Visual Schedules

Simple visual schedules need only two components:

- A visual symbol for each step (line drawings, clip art, photographs, pictures, words)
- A medium for displaying the symbols in sequence (tag board, construction paper, pocket chart, manila folder, chalkboard, whiteboard, laminated paper, photo album, etc.)

Some activities may also require a means for the child to indicate the process has been completed—perhaps a folder for finished assignments, or a box for completed projects.

How to Use Visual Schedules

Once the visual schedule has been completed, you or a volunteer can review it with the child and allow time for practice. The child may also want to practice storing the schedule so it can be easily accessed when it's needed again. Wait until the child is familiar and comfortable with one visual schedule before introducing a new one. To find more examples of visual schedules and learn more about how to use them, check out the resources below.

Visual Schedule Resources and Ideas

Boardmaker Software: http://www.mayer-johnson.com/boardmaker-software

Downloadable Visuals: http://connectability.ca/visuals-engine/

Tips and Ideas for Making Visual Schedules: http://challengingbehavior.fmhi.usf.edu/explore/pbs_docs/tips_for_visuals.pdf

Visual Schedule Ideas on Pinterest: http://www.pinterest.com/aacandat/visual-schedules/

Visual Schedules: http://www.gvsu.edu/cms3/assets/2CF6CA25-D6C6-F19E-339DC5CD2EB1B543/secondarylevellinkprograms/visual_schedules.docx

Chapter 3

Appetizers: Strategies to Prepare Children for Learning

Can you remember a time when you were a visitor at someone's home, and they served a main dish you'd never seen or tasted before? You didn't know whether to let it cool, eat it hot, devour it whole, or cut it open. Even after observing what other people did and copying them, you still worried. Would it taste delicious or disgusting? Would you get it down without making a fool of yourself? "Oh," you wished, "if only the hostess had served this unusual dish as a small appetizer and demonstrated how to eat it, I might have enjoyed myself."

In this chapter, you'll learn ways to introduce new environments, new processes, and new concepts to children in small, appetizing ways. These strategies show how to engage every child—even the ones who come earlier than you expected—the minute they walk in the door. One shows how to use charts to give kids a taste of the lesson and whet their appetites for learning. Others demonstrate how to use book walks and pre-reading strategies to cut concepts into bite-sized pieces for easy digestion and enjoyment.

A Prayer for Preparing Children to Learn

*Lord, some children consider this place a comfortable home
away from home. For others it feels like a foreign land.
Give me a heart sensitive to their needs. Help me make this
an appetizing, loving place, filled with the aroma of Christ,
so they can taste and see that You are good.*

Strategy 1—Sponge Activities

Wouldn't it be lovely if every child arrived at Sunday school at precisely the same time? Just imagine—all of your students filing into the room in quiet, orderly fashion, ready to begin the first activity.

Anyone who has ever volunteered to teach Sunday school knows that this never happens. Planning lessons, therefore, means that we have to plan not only the Bible story, music and projects, but also every moment our students spend in our care—from the moment they enter the church until they go home.

What Are Sponge Activities?

The time between kids' arrivals and the start of the lesson requires careful attention. We've all experienced down time that has deteriorated into chaos. As one sage teacher noted, "Kids get into trouble when they don't know what they're supposed to do." Therefore, when children arrive, be sure they have activities to engage them right away. Sometimes called sponge activities, these games or projects are designed to soak up the extra time before a lesson.

How to Prepare Sponge Activities

Fortunately, sponge activities don't require a tremendous amount of preparation. Consider the ideas below to determine what might work for your class:

- *Coloring or activity sheets.* Select ones that support the concepts you'll be discussing or that have been covered in recent weeks.
- *Puzzles.* If space permits, choose a large puzzle that can remain on a table in the room. This way, students can work on it from week to week.
- *Greeting cards.* Kids can create cards for church members' birthdays, pastors, missionaries, or those who are struggling with illness.

- *Card games or board games.* Again, select those that reinforce Bible concepts or ones that are fun and promote taking turns, conversation, and friendship.
- *Classroom jobs.* Assign children to be greeters, paper passers, craft table stockers, or book organizers.
- *Treasure hunts.* Hide pennies or other objects throughout the room and have children try to find, but not gather, them.
- *Reading corner.* Encourage kids who enjoy reading to curl up with a good book.
- *Videos.* Have a curriculum-related video playing as children come in.

We want students to feel welcome and nurtured from the moment they arrive. Sponge activities provide gentle structure as well as some creativity and fun, and allow them to absorb information as well.

Strategy 2—The Weekly News: A Welcoming Activity

As most church folks know, arriving on time for scheduled children's ministry events can be difficult, especially for families affected by disabilities. Often, this means that kids arrive before the lesson starts, creating an unstructured beginning to the hour. As was mentioned before, professionals call this sponge time. One sponge time solution is "The Weekly News."

- Using a large piece of chart paper divided into sections, you can create a mock-up of a newspaper's front page. The sections can include World Events, Local Headlines, Health, Sports, Arts, Schools, Celebrations, and Concerns.
- As the children arrive, they can use sticky notes to add news to the chart paper. For example, one child can jot down details of her soccer matches and place it in the Sports section, while another can write about a band concert and put it in Arts. Kids can add upcoming tests or quizzes in the School section or details about a sick grandparent in Health. By using sticky notes, the children can each work on their piece of news without having to crowd at the chart paper all at once.
- Once everyone arrives, you can use your Weekly News to focus conversation and prepare for prayer time. This allows kids to pray purposefully for each other, using the chart for reference.

- The stickies can be distributed at the end of your time together as a reminder to pray for specific requests during the week.

This activity provides a meaningful activity that engages children as soon as they enter the room. In addition, it sets the stage for kids to learn more about each other so they can form relationships with church friends.

Strategy 3—"Looks Like, Sounds Like, Feels Like" Charts

The first time many kids with special needs enter a Sunday school classroom or other children's ministry program space, they experience considerable fear and trepidation. They may not know how to act. They may not be able to make their bodies respond the way they should. They may become frustrated because behavior expectations for the lesson are quite different from expectations for game time, bathroom breaks, or the craft table.

A "Looks Like, Sounds Like, Feels Like" chart created with students can make meeting behavioral expectations easier for three reasons. First, the teacher creates the chart with students, coaching them along the way with concrete examples. Second, after making the chart the kids also practice the expectations. Third, kids can refer to the chart when they aren't sure how to behave.

To make the chart, copy the sample chart in Appendix C (page 169). You can also enlarge the graphics, cut them out, and paste them onto a larger piece of construction paper or tagboard. Above the graphics, write the title. (Examples: Story Time, Game Time, Bathroom Break, Craft Table)

Now you're ready to complete the chart with your students. Let's say you're discussing story time behavior. Tell the children in clear, general terms what's expected during story time. For example, you might say: "During story time, look at the person telling or reading the story. Sit quietly on your carpet square. When you have a question or something to say, raise your hand. Then wait until you are called upon to speak."

Then ask the children, "What will story time look like? What would someone looking in the window of our room see you doing?" Depending on their ages and abilities, write or draw the children's responses in the correct columns of the chart. Once that is done, ask, "What will story time sound like? If someone closed his eyes, what would he or she hear?" Record those responses, and move on to "What will story time feel like? What would someone sitting like you're sitting feel?" Once the chart is finished, read it together, pausing to practice and notice how each behavior looks sounds and feels. Finally, hang the chart on the classroom wall or bulletin board so children can refer to it.

New charts can be created as needed for a variety of scenarios. But make no more than one chart per class period or session, since kids with special needs often require extra time to absorb new expectations. Post charts where they can be easily seen and referred to during the activity described.

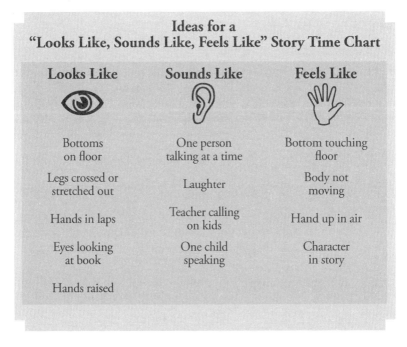

Ideas for a
"Looks Like, Sounds Like, Feels Like" Story Time Chart

Looks Like	Sounds Like	Feels Like
Bottoms on floor	One person talking at a time	Bottom touching floor
Legs crossed or stretched out	Laughter	Body not moving
Hands in laps	Teacher calling on kids	Hand up in air
Eyes looking at book	One child speaking	Character in story
Hands raised		

Strategy 4—Know/Wonder/Learn (KWL) Charts

Teaching new concepts to students in school, youth group, or on Sunday mornings, can be a daunting task. Students bring with them a variety of background experiences, varying levels of knowledge and interest, as well as unique personalities and needs. We need to focus every student's attention on the subject matter and modify the lesson on the spot in order to meet the needs of the group.

How to Create KWL Charts

One strategy to make this task easier is a Know/Wonder/Learn (KWL) chart. By using this tool, we tap into the students' background knowledge, prepare them for the lesson ahead, and assess their learning. And this strategy requires virtually no prep time nor materials. It can be used for both factual information and concepts such as love, sacrifice, and forgiveness.

To make a KWL chart, create a three-columned chart on a piece of chart paper, chalkboard, or whiteboard. At the top of the chart, write the subject that the group will be studying. In this example, we'll talk about Moses.

Share What We *Know*

Ask the children, "What do we *know* about Moses? " As they begin to respond, write their statements on the chart paper. For example, they might say, "His mom put him in a basket in the river," or "He was a leader," or even "He made up the Ten Commandments." This step serves several purposes:

- It introduces the concept and the purpose of the lesson to children.
- It helps children access background knowledge. When they do this, they are more likely to remember and apply the new information they will receive.
- It serves as an assessment tool. You can gauge the students' understanding and also be aware of any misconceptions the students might have, such as "He made up the Ten Commandments."

If other students question a statement, the teacher can simply say, "I wondered that, too. Let's just put a question mark there so that we can check all of our facts for accuracy." This step also allows the teacher to model kindness, good group discussion etiquette, and turn-taking.

Share What We *Wonder*

Now, focus the group on the next section of the chart by asking, "What do we *wonder* about this topic?" As children formulate questions, record them on the chart. Creating questions about a topic is a higher-level language skill. You can model this by thinking aloud and saying, "I wonder what Moses said to God when he was praying?" or "When did Moses know he was supposed to be a leader?"

Writing *who, what, when, where, why* and *how* on the top of this section can help students to ask similar questions. This stage of the strategy sets anticipation for active learning. The kids are now on a mission to find the answers to their questions.

Share New Information to *Learn*

Now that the children are ready to learn, review their questions and remind them to listen for answers. Next, present the information by reading the Bible—or for some classes, have children read aloud to the group, or silently to themselves. Then, return to the chart and list the facts *learned* in the third column.

How to Gently Correct Misconceptions

When correcting a child's misconception, try these phrases to emphasize learning as a lifelong process and the church as a safe and supportive place to learn:

- "That was a little confusing. I'm glad that we could learn together."
- "I learned a lot today; some of my ideas about Moses weren't exactly what the Bible tells me."

During this stage, have children look at the first column and correct any inconsistencies. For example, "We just learned that Moses didn't make up the Ten Commandments. God did! And Moses helped the people learn the commandments." This final step allows teachers to assess the students' new knowledge and also begin the planning process for the next lesson.

Strategy 5—Take a Walk: A Book Walk

Of all the activities that comprise Sunday school time, Bible stories are perhaps the most important. After all, the sixty-six books of the Bible reveal God's story, His instructions, and His love for His children. In addition, the Bible provides guidance for making choices, praying, and interacting with others. We certainly want our time spent in the Word to be productive and enriching for students.

However, sitting and listening to a Bible story can be quite difficult for many kids with disabilities. They may struggle to maintain attention or be unable to process new information effectively. One activity to increase kids' comprehension and memory for Bible stories is a Book Walk. This strategy takes only a few minutes, and requires a little planning, but can enhance the listening experience for all learners.

- Introduce the story: "Today, we're going to read about a man named Zacchaeus."
- Show the students the title of the story, and read it aloud: "Zacchaeus Wants to Meet Jesus."
- Comment or ask a question about the title to get kids thinking about the topic: "I wonder why he was so interested in meeting Jesus." Or, "Zacchaeus sure is an interesting name. I don't think he was a disciple, so I wonder who he was?"
- Flip through the pages of the story, commenting and asking questions so the children can formulate predictions: "My goodness, he is climbing a tree! I wonder why he is doing that? What will Jesus think when he sees Zacchaeus up there?"
- Ask the students to make predictions. "What do you think Zacchaeus will do? What might he say if he meets Jesus?"
- Read boldface words or subheadings: "This word in bold print is tax collector. I wonder if that was an important job. I wonder why it is important in this story."
- Segue from the Book Walk to the story. "Okay, we've definitely got some ideas of what we might read. Let's see what the Bible tells us about Zacchaeus."
- After reading, ask questions: "Which of our predictions about Zacchaeus were correct? What did you learn that you didn't know before?"

This strategy helps children actively participate in the story, and it allows them to anticipate what they might learn. This usually results in stronger comprehension, increasing the likelihood that the story remains in students' minds and in their hearts as well.

Strategy 6—Pre-Reading Strategies: Prepare for Success

Pre-reading strategies, including Book Walks, are precisely what their name implies. They are strategies to employ before reading aloud to kids, before asking them to read information or a story on their own, or before asking them to complete a worksheet that contains paragraphs of written text. Jolene used to tell her students that pre-reading strategies were magic tricks, because when properly used ahead of time, they made the work of reading much, much easier. Almost like magic.

Pre-reading is a way to "front-load" the brain. It allows children to explore the topic, become familiar with the vocabulary, and get an idea of where the material is going before they engage in the heavy lifting of reading the text. It's an important strategy for all children, but it can be vital to the success of kids with special needs. Here are some ways to expand its use beyond Book Walks to Sunday school papers and chapter books as children get older and reading material becomes more complicated.

- *Read the title* together and talk about it before children read the text. Ask children what they think the title means.
- *Look at pictures* accompanying the title. Ask if the pictures confirm their ideas or if they need to make adjustments.
- *Have children find and read any headings* in the text. Again, ask what children think they mean. Then use pictures on the page to confirm or adjust ideas. Do the same with picture captions.
- *Look for sidebars.* Read through them together, again making predictions and talking about how they relate to the title, headings, and pictures.
- *Instruct children to read the text* once you feel the kids are sufficiently front-loaded.
- *Repeat the process for each page* if the reading material is several pages long.

Keep in mind that many children benefit from pre-reading one day and reading the text on a different day. Somehow, the pre-reading discussion marinates their brain cells to make connections.

Some students may still struggle with reading text, even after pre-reading. Chapter 5 offers several reading strategies you can use so those students will experience reading success as they learn about Jesus.

Chapter 4

Every Child Welcome:
Creating a Positive
Classroom Culture

W hat's the difference between a dinner party soon forgotten and a gathering you'd like to attend again and again? In many cases, what draws us back is a welcoming atmosphere, a sense of belonging, and the opportunity to engage in conversation without fear of negative reactions from others. We want the children who come to our church to experience a similar atmosphere. Therefore, we need to create a positive classroom climate.

This chapter is packed with strategies, resources, and activities that promote a positive climate. Implementing these ideas takes time and energy, but every iota invested into creating a positive atmosphere will reap big dividends. Kids will want to return because they feel secure, and they belong. They will learn to show the compassion and kindness of Christ because they experience His compassion and kindness each time they walk through the door. So invest heavily in the activities related in this chapter and be prepared to reap rich rewards.

A Prayer for Compassion

*Jesus, be in this place. Let Your compassion and kindness
permeate every activity planned. Give me the ability to
model compassion, patience, and love. Open the hearts of
the children present, so they sense Your love for them, so they
know that they belong to You. Make them feel welcome so
they will return and learn about You time after time.*

Strategy 1—Inclusion Is Not a Place

Pastors and volunteers often want to know how to keep kids
with special needs in the same room as their typically developing
peers. Many strategies exist to accomplish this. However, there's a
bigger issue to be tackled. When we think of inclusion as a physical
place within a building, we're missing out on what it truly means.
Inclusion has to be more than just geography. It has to be cardiology:
studied and felt in the heart.

The Right Fit

When planning for inclusion, we need to consider each child's
strengths and needs so that we can determine the most appropriate supports. Think of it this way: Determining how to include and
support a student is rather like choosing a pair of pants. We don't
want our pants too tight, and we don't want them too loose. We desire that "just right" fit. Not everyone is a size 2 or 10 or 22W. In order to be comfortable and able to attend to our work, we want pants
that fit our own curves.

Let's apply this to a church setting. Not every child will be comfortable participating in every aspect of the typical Sunday school setting.
That size may not fit every child—and that is okay. Our goal for inclusion is to find the right fit so we can be certain that the child and family
are fully included in the life of the church.

Strategy 2—Finding the Right Fit for Every Child

As we plan for inclusion, we need to ensure the following:

- We, as the church, must accept that some kids might need a
  break or a different activity or even, at times, an alternative
  activity or space.

- We need to be sure that we include kids with their peers to the greatest extent that is possible and comfortable for the child. A special needs diagnosis should not dictate the supports and placement of the child. The child's strengths, needs and preferences should inform these decisions.
- We must find and use the gifts of every kid to advance the kingdom.
- We need to be flexible, creative, and supportive so that kids can enjoy and contribute to age-appropriate programming that's meaningful.
- Volunteers and pastors maintain an attitude of true inclusion, reflecting one body with many parts. Everyone is necessary and everyone has gifts.
- We must plan prayerfully and respectfully, creating experiences that are based on kids' strengths and needs, not on diagnoses and labels.

Finally, remember that providing the right fit does not mean that students need to be separated from typically developing peers. On the contrary, this is an opportunity for some special friendships to develop. Consider inviting a few friends to join a child or small group of kids with special needs in a separate setting. This allows kids to enjoy each other's company in a structured, well-paced situation. These kinds of experiences allow typically developing kids to appreciate the gifts and talents of kids they might not otherwise know, a sure way to build the church family for eternity. Inclusion isn't a place—it's the body of Christ.

Strategy 3—Including the Most Valuable Player (MVP)

When adults put their heads together to plan for kids, great things usually happen. However, we need to be sure we include the most valuable human player: the child. But wait, you might be saying, we need to leave the decision-making up to the adults. After all, they know best.

Benefits for the MVP

There's truth to that statement; adults do have wisdom and perspective when it comes to educational or church planning. However, when we include MVPs, we accomplish some important things:

- Children are encouraged to understand themselves better.
- Children learn that pastors and teachers are approachable and available.
- Children have more buy-in to the programs because they feel a measure of participation and control.

Benefits for the Kingdom

When we include children, we lay the foundation for lifelong spiritual growth. Each child in our church has unique and special talents and strengths. As parents, pastors, and teachers, part of our job is to help kids understand and appreciate their own strengths so they can use them for the kingdom. In addition, we can help students identify their areas of weakness, and then demonstrate support and encouragement in those areas. In short, we teach our MVPs that every member of the body is useful and necessary.

How to Involve the MVPs

So, how can we accomplish this? Children and youth—with or without disabilities—have varying levels of ability to understand and communicate their strengths and needs. However, the adults in the child's life can ease the process by creating meaningful opportunities for the child to interact with the pastors or teachers.

- Have children create pictures of themselves (depending on skill levels, create artwork rather than a self-portrait) to give to the pastors.
- Take photographs and help children send them via email to the church staff or teacher, along with a note of introduction or a list of strengths or needs.
- Use the "Let Me Introduce Myself" template (see Appendix B, page 167) with children who can dictate answers or can write them independently. Send their creations to church staff and teachers.

Bear in mind, MVP activities are not appropriate for all children and circumstances. That's okay. We don't want to press children or youth into disclosing needs in a way that would embarrass them or deter their participation. It is, however, an excellent opportunity to model communication about our own strengths and needs. If we do so with honesty and humility, kids will often follow our lead in healthy and productive ways. Power to the (little) people!

Strategy 4—Focusing on Strengths Rather Than Needs

The parents sank into the comfortable couches in the pastor's office. They had scheduled a time to explain their son's autism, and create a plan for his participation in church.

"So great to see you," the pastor said. "Thanks for coming in."

The parents smiled, the weariness evident in their eyes.

"So," said the pastor, "tell me what's wonderful about your son."

Silence.

The parents looked at each other, a mixture of bewilderment, gratitude, and grief crossing their countenances. Tears welled up in their eyes, and a sob from deep in the mother's throat escaped.

Finally, the father spoke. "No one ever asks us that anymore," he whispered. "Everyone just wants to talk about his problems. His bad behavior. His inability to speak. No one ever asks about his strengths."

Every Child Has Strengths

Every child has strengths. Some kids are athletic. Some love to sing. Others enjoy helping or praying or creating. It's often easy to identify gifts and talents in students who are typically developing. However, when we work with kids who have disabilities, our focus quickly shifts to what's wrong, and we ask, "How can I help you?" Our intentions are good, and we absolutely need to know what we can do to support and assist. Still, we need to cultivate a strengths-focused culture.

Strategies that Focus on a Child's Strengths

By identifying and actively using the strengths of the children in our program, we send a strong message that the body of Christ needs every member. We also help kids to find common interests and appreciate the gifts of others. Finally, we demonstrate strongly that our church's focus is markedly different than that of the secular world. As you welcome children into your program, find their strengths using these strategies:

- Add a line to your registration form that asks, "What are your child's strengths?"
- Observe students during class with a focus on finding strengths. Do you notice generosity in a student? Does a child demonstrate leadership or compassion?
- Discover ways to use those gifts for the good of the church or community. How can you utilize a child's coordination or

artistic abilities? Could children with a gift for hospitality join the greeting team?

- Help children to find others with similar gifts and also express appreciation for those with talents unlike their own.

A church culture that emphasizes strengths does more than build self-esteem. It builds the kingdom.

Strategy 5—Rules to Live By: Creating Classroom Rules

Kids hate rules. At least, that's what they say. But deep down, kids love rules. They crave the security created by reasonable rules that are consistently maintained. Those kinds of rules show them what to expect from others and how to behave themselves. No matter how often kids say they hate rules, their church experience will feel safer and be more fun if the rules are clearly stated and enforced.

Kids are more willing to live by rules they help establish. So spend a few minutes at the beginning of your first meeting time to create a short list of rules. First, discuss why rules are needed: They keep us safe; they explain how to act; they teach right and wrong; they make it possible to learn and have fun. Next, ask children to brainstorm rules. Write their suggestions on the sticky notes and place them on a piece of chart paper, the wall, or a whiteboard. Then, have the children group similar rules into three to five groups or clusters.

Finally—and this is the tricky part—look at the clusters and write one broad rule for each one. Confused? Don't be. As you use this strategy, you'll discover the ideas brainstormed by kids settle into a few broad categories:

- Speaking
- Listening
- Respect and compassion for others
- Safety
- Obeying the adult in charge

So one group of suggestions will contain ideas on the order of, "don't talk while someone else is talking, let other people talk, don't hog the conversation, be quiet." Your job is to craft those into one sentence encompassing the spirit of all the suggestions. Try to use positive language like "Raise your hand to speak and wait to be called on." That tells kids much more about what they should do than "Don't talk until you have permission." Also, use language churched and unchurched kids can understand. Choose "Treat others like you want to be treated" over "Follow the golden rule."

Before the next time kids come, write all the rules on a large piece of tagboard. When they arrive for the next session, read through the rules together. Practice each rule a few times. Then, ask the children to sign the chart if they agree to abide by the rules. Once that's done, post the rules prominently in the classroom or meeting area.

For the first month—or whenever there's a large influx of new children—review the rules and practice them again. And always remember to enforce the rules wisely and compassionately. Before long, the rules will become habit and the kids will forget the chart is there. But leave it up anyway because the kids helped make it, and it's presence on the wall reminds them that their voices have been heard.

> **Three Tips for Positive Classroom Rules**
>
> - Create three to five broad rules.
> - Use positive language.
> - Use kid language.

Strategy 6—Creating Security with Classroom Routines

The security of a child's world is built upon habit and routine. Secure babies know someone comforts them when they cry. Young children thrive when parents establish routines for bath time, bedtime, mealtime, and more. The confidence of school-aged children increases when they know what to expect throughout the day. And kids on the autism spectrum and with behavioral special needs function best with a routine. Therefore, part of cultivating a positive classroom or program climate is to establish and maintain a consistent routine. Doing so requires a little planning before your program begins, training and practicing with kids when they arrive, and anticipating inevitable changes in the routine.

Advance Planning

Before your first class session, create a schedule and write it on the whiteboard or chart paper. (See *Schedules: Helping Kids Know What to Expect,* page 39.) Then think through every step of your time together and ask questions about the routines associated with each step. Where will kids put coats? Where will supplies be stored and how will kids access them? What is the bathroom usage procedure? What is the dismissal policy?

Training and Practice

Once children arrive, explain the schedule to them. Take them on a tour of the classroom, pointing out where to hang coats and where supplies are stored. Then, refer to the schedule to see what's next and move on. While transitioning from one activity to the next, explain the routine, and let kids practice a time or two. During your first few meetings, draw the kids' attention to the schedule and review routines so they can get used to them. Once things are running smoothly, revisit the schedule and practice routines only when the kids need a refresher.

Anticipating Changes in Routine

Even the most scrupulously established and maintained routines sometimes break down. Christmas pageant practice swallows November and December Sunday school. Bad weather delays a program's start time. Camp Promotion Sunday usurps class time. These changes threaten the security of some kids whose love of routine makes them inflexible. They need time to process upcoming change so they can switch gears. These strategies are designed to give them the time they need to adjust to changes in routine:

- If you know about the change in advance, discuss it with the child before dismissal time. Write out the adjusted schedule and send it home so the child can study it during the week.
- Some children may respond better hearing about the change from their parents. In that case send parents an email several days ahead of time, outlining the schedule change, or discuss it in a phone call so they can talk to their kids.
- When there's little advance warning, create a new schedule. Use a picture schedule for non-readers if necessary. (See *Visual Schedules: The Eyes Have It*, page 40.) Then put the schedule where the child can see it before entering the classroom—in her cubby, on the wall where she hangs her coat, or give it to her buddy so they can go to a quiet place and review it. Give the child time to process the changes and then join the group.

> **Helpful Hint**
>
> *Kids on the autism spectrum often feel more secure sitting near the schedule. If that's the case, rearrange the seating chart so they can look at it for reassurance whenever they want.*

Creating and maintaining classroom routines allows kids with special needs to function at their best. And because childhood security is built upon habit and routine, all kids will benefit from children's ministry programs with well-established classroom routines.

Strategy 7—Peer Training

Her chin quivered, and her eyes filled with tears. "The school year wasn't very good," she confided. "He went through the whole year without making one friend."

Sadly, this mother's statement is quite common. Children with disabilities are frequently left out of play dates, birthday parties, and afternoons at the pool. The isolation is felt by the entire family. Neighbors and acquaintances, unsure of how to manage a child's needs, may be reluctant to include families at barbecues or block parties.

Benefits of Peer Training

One of the best methods for curing this loneliness is peer training. An abundant natural resource in church programs, typically developing peers possess great potential for improving inclusion. By offering training for peers on how to help and interact with their friends who have disabilities, all children benefit.

Peer training has long been a component of social skills intervention in public schools. Educators note that when properly implemented, buddy programs provide several benefits. Children with disabilities show increased eye contact and conversational skills. In addition, they report feeling more confident in their social interactions, and they are less likely to play alone at recess time.

The benefits extend to the typically developing peers as well. Many show improved leadership skills and an improved ability to understand and accept those who are different. Moreover, these buddy programs might prevent typical kids from developing bully behavior.

Finally, strong peer training builds an increased sense of community and responsibility. Fortunately, this extends beyond one school year and, therefore, has positive effects as students get older. Parents of kids with disabilities express their appreciation, believing that friendships are an important part of their child's development.

Direct Peer Training

In order to set kids up for success, provide some direct training. A short training session can include:

- Basic information about disabilities
- Safety rules
- Polite ways to offer help
- When to ask a teacher for help
- Ways to communicate

Specific Peer Information

While basic training will be important, a peer buddy program is most effective when kids can receive specific information about the child with whom they will be paired. Saying, "Kids with autism have difficulty with eye contact" is good. But it's more helpful to say, "When Jacob is talking, he usually won't look you in the eye. It doesn't mean he doesn't like you, it just helps him to focus on what he is saying."

Another example: "People who have cerebral palsy might walk or talk differently than you do" can be a starting point, but this is more helpful: "When Mario walks, he might go slowly. And, when he is having a conversation, it takes some time to get his words out. It might be hard to understand him at first, but you will catch on quickly. He has a lot of information about Harry Potter, just like you." Also, allow kids to observe their buddies, and reserve time for them to ask questions about them.

Importance of Peer Respect

Finally, strongly emphasize respect. Children who volunteer as buddies will need clear guidance on how to respect their new friends' feelings. Buddies should understand the importance of using positive words and refusing to gossip about their new friends.

Another way to encourage respectful relationships between peers is to offer some interest groups. Perhaps some kids who enjoy video games can meet once each month, or those who like art can bring their projects and work together. This allows kids to notice that often, they have more in common than they think, which can be the start of authentic, lasting friendships.

We want kids to make friends and work together while they're at church. After all, we're the body of Christ, and learning how to collaborate is an important part of a healthy body. However, all kids benefit from some instruction on how to work cooperatively. Students who have disabilities that affect language and social skills might need additional support. In the next few sections, we'll discuss why working with a partner or group might be difficult, and how we can make it easier for everyone.

Strategy 8—Pick a Partner, Part 1 Understanding Why Working Together Might Be Hard

As teachers or volunteer leaders in churches, we encourage students to collaborate and work together. It's an important skill and a necessary one. However, students with hidden disabilities often struggle with this type of activity. For them, the three most frightening words uttered by teachers are *find a partner*. These kids are all too familiar with the feeling of being chosen last for a study group, or not being chosen at all.

Often, students with hidden disabilities lack the skills necessary to work effectively with a partner or small group. Reasons for this are many:

- *Poor impulse control.* Students may blurt out answers, talk about irrelevant topics or leave the group to work on something else.
- *Difficulties with taking turns.* Students might interrupt their peers or demand the first turn and become angry when they don't get it.
- *Social anxiety.* Working in a group can be so stressful that it causes physical symptoms, such as an upset stomach, racing heart, or sweating. Students who experience this might be unable to take part because they feel unwell.
- *Problems with expressive language.* Sometimes, students have difficulty retrieving information at the same speed as their peers; they need extra time to collect their thoughts.
- *Struggles with perspective-taking.* Working in pairs or groups requires cooperation, and that means being able to understand another person's perspective. This sophisticated skill can be elusive for many students with hidden disabilities.
- *Difficulty with task completion.* When students work in groups, they often need to complete tasks at home. Students with hidden disabilities sometimes struggle with organization and task completion.
- *Low frustration tolerance.* Sometimes, students with hidden disabilities are quick to become upset or angry when the group does not agree with their ideas, or when they perceive that the work is not going according to plan. When this happens, they may become frustrated and angry with their peers. They might also have difficulty regulating their emotions.
- *Uneven skill development.* Sometimes, students with disabilities may be very capable in some academic areas, but have tremen-

dous difficulty in others. When a group assignment requires them to perform in a less-developed skill set, they may be embarrassed and reluctant to participate.

The good news? These students can—and should—work in pairs and small groups. But, they need explicit instruction in order to be successful. In truth, every student benefits from such instruction. Therefore, we need to plan the students' interactions just as carefully as we plan our own teaching.

Strategy 9—Pick a Partner, Part 2
Strategies for Making It Work Well

For some students with disabilities, working with others can be challenging. However, the skills necessary to cooperate with peers, share ideas, and work on a common goal provide the foundation for long-term participation in the church. We can shape these behaviors with careful planning. Here are some planning strategies to make that happen.

Think It Through
An old adage says, "If you fail to plan, you plan to fail." The danger with this, for teachers, is that lack of planning on the teacher's part can result in failure for the students. Therefore, teachers need to define objects for both the product and the process. By clearly defining the end-results for product and process, teachers provide structure and purpose (see example below).

Example of How to Define Product and Process

Define the Product: By working in a small group, students will create a booklet that summarizes the story they have read.

Define the Process: As they work in groups, students will take turns sharing ideas without interrupting.

Do Some Choreography
Just as a choreographer plans each move of a dance, we must plan for group work. Moving from individual or large group work to small group work takes tremendous energy and concentration for many students. While some students move easily to new activities, students with hidden disabilities may face several hurdles such as following multi-step

directions, difficulty moving through a crowd without bumping into others, or anxiety at the change of activity.

Therefore, it's critically important for teachers to plan where groups will sit, how the students move through the room, and what directions will be given to minimize confusion. For example:

> "Pick up your pencil and markers. When you're ready, look at me. Students in Group A can now stand and walk to the story corner." (Wait until Group A is seated.) "Great! Group B students can stand and walk to the art table."

Create Boundaries

Group work allows students some freedom to explore ideas and collaborate. However, this freedom requires boundaries and structure to ensure student success. Teachers can set students up for success by providing parameters that help productivity.

- *A checklist* for the components of the project provides a visual reminder of the directions, and moves children through the task.
- *A bell or chime* prompts children to move through the activity and supports task completion.
- *Visual timers* (see page 101) can also encourage better time management for those with a poor sense of time.

With all of the planning necessary for group work, it may seem easier to plan a teacher-directed lesson. However, the opportunity for students to take charge of their learning—and learn from and with each other—makes this behind-the-scenes planning worth all the effort.

Strategy 10—Pick a Partner, Part 3
More Strategies for Making This Work Well

Do you remember the reality show *The Apprentice*? On this program, groups of entrepreneurs or celebrities work together on tasks in the hopes of eventually being named Donald Trump's apprentice. As with most reality shows, it's chock-full of drama, stemming mainly from the friction between team members. The group dynamics frequently ignite a firestorm of arguments.

The problem, it often seems, is that the groups had very little time to talk about how they were going to work together. They're immediately thrust into managing tasks; getting to know one another and establishing norms for the group are often considered irrelevant. The result? Misunderstandings, hurt feelings, errors, and incomplete work.

As we consider group activities for kids with disabilities, we need to remember this bit of wisdom: *Be ye not so rushed.* The time we invest in helping all kids learn how to work together will pay huge dividends, not only in student achievement, but also in social/emotional development. More importantly, we're helping kids to understand more fully how to be the body of Christ. Here are some steps for helping students work together:

Create rules. Before we allow children in the worship center or on the playground, we give them a set of expectations to keep them safe and to help them manage their interactions. The same logic applies to group work. In an interview with veteran teacher Sheri Halagan, Sheri notes, "Kids don't know as much as we think they know about how to behave." We need to remember, too, that some students with hidden disabilities struggle with social skills and thrive on structure and rules. Before starting group work, gather the class together and facilitate a discussion about rules that should govern the tasks and interactions.

Reinforce the rules. As teachers and volunteers who work with children and teens, we're constantly reviewing and reteaching. Anything we teach, from subtraction to science to Scripture, must be reinforced so it can be remembered. In the same way, we need to review the social curriculum for students so they can internalize how to interact with each other in a positive and productive way. Classroom consultant Margaret Berry Wilson writes in her blog "Bringing Rules to Life":

> It is important to keep discussing and practicing the rules all year long. Students cannot possibly learn all they need to about how to live and behave as a community during the first weeks of school. Time spent together deepens their understanding of how to truly care for each other. Also, keeping the rules alive and ever-present in children's minds gives you the ability to ask "What do our rules say about . . . ?" when challenging situations arise.[1]

These comments readily apply not only to the classroom in school, but also to church as well. In both settings, students need consistent, kind reminders about the rules that govern positive teamwork.

---

1. https://www.responsiveclassroom.org/blog/bringing-rules-life, accessed February 3, 2014.

Strategy 11—The Power of
Story in Explaining Special Needs

One component of creating a positive culture for kids of kindergarten age and older is to discuss special needs together. Unless the topic is addressed, kids will create their own explanations—based on their limited knowledge and hallway hearsay—about why some children act certain ways, look different, walk different, use a wheelchair, or make unusual noises. And until the topic is addressed, children have no idea of how to respond to a classmate who doesn't act the way same-age peers do.

Tell a Story

Often, group effort is required to maintain the dignity of a child with special needs. Invite the parents to be part of the group. Since they have probably dealt with this issue before, they may have useful suggestions. Parents of a child with diabetes may agree to talk to the kids about the disease, demonstrate how blood sugar is tested, and what to do if their child begins acting strangely. Others may do a wheelchair demonstration with their child, or explain the tubes and machines connected to a child who is medically fragile. When parents and child are comfortable telling their family's story and fielding questions afterward, peers usually become more welcoming and inclusive.

However, the above scenario isn't always possible. Some parents and kids aren't comfortable speaking in front of a group. Telling some special needs stories in front of the child can be awkward or inappropriate. In those cases, ask parents for permission to have another adult (the child's assigned buddy, another volunteer, or the children's ministry leader) to work with the child in a different setting while you or the parents talk to the other children. Then use kid-friendly language to tell the story of the child's special needs condition. Suggest ways peers can include the child and how to respond to behaviors. Leave time for them to ask questions, too. Careful attention to their questions will reveal their level of understanding and what more needs to be addressed.

Read a Story

Another effective way to approach the topic is by reading books about kids with special needs to children. Reading a story allows them to observe and process from a comfortable distance and often leads to rich discussion. Before reading the story, prepare kids by linking what will be read to something they already know.

For example, after a lesson about how every person in God's creation is unique, you could begin the discussion with, "We just talked about how we're all different and unique. In this story we'll meet some of God's very unique kids." While reading the story, stop now and then to ask questions and comment about the pictures. When the story is finished, let kids talk about how characters in the story felt, discuss the lesson of the story, and how to apply it to their own lives.

Several excellent children's books are listed in the sidebar. But new books come out every year. To keep up-to-date with new titles, call the director of the children's section of your public library or the librarian at the nearest elementary school. They love books and love to share their favorite finds with others.

Susan Laughs by Jeanne Willis and Tony Ross (Henry Holt and Co., 2000) Preschool–second

Don't Call Me Special: A First Look at Disability by Pat Thomas (Barron's Educational Series, 2005) Preschool & up

Special People, Special Ways by Arlene Maguire (Future Horizons, 2000) Kindergarten & up

Thank You, Mr Falker by Patricia Polacco (Philomel, 2012) Kindergarten & up

In Jesse's Shoes: Appreciating Kids with Special Needs by Beverly Lewis (Bethany House, 2007) Primary & up

My Brother Charlie by Holly Robinson Peete (Scholastic Press, 2010) Second–fifth

Just the Way I Am: God's Good Design in Disability by Krista Horning (Christian Focus Publications, 2011) Second–fifth

Strategy 12—Creating a Meaningful Plan for Each Child at Church

Good teaching takes good planning. Any curriculum guide or teaching manual clearly outlines the best ways to prepare for lessons. The federal government thinks planning is a good idea, too. In fact, every public school student who is identified with a disability that affects learning has a plan called an Individualized Education Plan (IEP). This plan lists the child's strengths, needs, and current levels of performance. In addition, the plan, formulated by teachers and school staff, includes goals and objectives that create the basis for the child's school year. Finally, the plan includes all of the supports, accommodations, and related services the child needs in order to make appropriate progress toward the identified goals. Every member of the child's team—including the child, when appropriate—works on this plan, signs it, and helps to monitor the child's progress.

So, if a student needs an IEP at school, then we should definitely have one at church, right? Not necessarily. Churches don't operate by the same legal standards as the schools, nor are they obligated to meet a student's individual learning objectives. Furthermore, the focus of church is not to improve academic skills or provide therapeutic support. However, churches do have a mandate to include every child in the Great Commission.

Our ministry colleague, Harmony Hensley often says, "Our God is a God of order; we show His love when we plan effectively!" So we do need a plan, but the type of plan and the process by which we implement it depends on many factors.

It Depends on the Parents

Some parents are very eager to share their child's needs with church staff, and want to collaborate with the team about goals for church. Others just want their child, as much as possible, to blend in with everyone else; they don't want the disability to be the focus at church. In this case, ministry leaders can provide necessary supports to help the child—and parents—enjoy their day of rest.

It Depends on the Church Staff and Volunteers

Some churches might decide that part of their mission and ministry is to offer as much support as possible to families. We won't assume that these are big churches or churches with large budgets. Nor will we assume that churches that provide in-depth, individualized planning or therapeutic supports are better than those that don't. Every church should approach this issue by taking into account a number of factors, such as the church's culture, staffing, facilities, vision of the senior staff, and availability of volunteers.

It Depends on the Child

Some children are eager to accept help as they work toward goals. Others are just really ready for a day that's fun and not focused on improving skills. Many teens with disabilities don't want to have extra focus on their needs during youth group time. This is a normal and expected part of teen development, and we need to respect it.

It Depends on the Plan

We need to remember that the purpose of a plan at church will most likely be very different from a plan at school, because the purpose of church is different. However, the information kids are learning at church is far more important than anything that will be taught at school. Therefore, churches and families should work together to create a plan for every child's spiritual growth—not only for kids with special needs.

It Ultimately Depends on God

Before we plan anything, we really need to ask God what He thinks about our ministry and where He would like to see it go.

The counsel of the LORD stands forever,
The plans of His heart from generation to generation.
Psalm 33:11 (NASB)

The GROW Plan for Spiritual Development

Consider using the GROW Plan for Spiritual Development (see page 161) to facilitate the process. The easy format also allows parents, churches and students to develop shared expectations; when we communicate about what our hopes and plans are, we are more likely to develop strong relationships that facilitate growth.

Sometimes it's not what we say, but how we say it. On busy Sunday mornings, it's difficult to plan our words as carefully as we might like. However, our communication is an important component in building relationships with parents and kids. In the next few articles, you'll learn some common communication pitfalls as well as some strategies for improving conversations.

Strategy 13—Effective Communication, Part 1
The Minimizer

Wouldn't it be great if we had some magical contraption that would shrink our troubles? We could put our mortgage or tuition bills in there. Ah, instant relief! Or perhaps we could lure a bothersome boss or meddling in-law into our minimizing machine. Boom! Those folks would seem suddenly more manageable. It's fun to think about, isn't it?

The reality? Life just doesn't work that way for any of us. Sometimes our worries become Goliath-sized, rendering us incapable of felling the giant. We've often seen this kind of despair in parents with children who have special needs. New diagnoses, concerns about academic and social development, regression of skills and stigmatizing behavior elicit fear for parents, causing grief and anxiety.

Well-meaning friends and family members try to soothe parents by taking on the role of *the minimizer*. In an effort to make the parent feel hopeful and comfortable, minimizers use phrases like this:

- Oh, don't worry about that behavior. All kids do that.
- His father was the same way, and he turned out just fine.
- You're making too much of this! It will be fine.
- She'll grow out of it.
- Oh, my nephew had that. It's no big deal.

Sound familiar? We've all said things like that to buoy the listener's spirit and allay the fears. In retrospect, doing so is like putting a bandage on the gaping wound. The verbal bandage made the speaker feel better for the moment, but the words weren't healing. They were frustrating.

Parents raising kids with behavioral disabilities know that all kids don't do that. Even if an exhibited behavior is typical, the accompanying difficulties can remind parents their circumstances are anything but typical. And that hurts. So what can we do?

- *Recognize that we are in a position to offer comfort and support.* Simply reflecting, "This is so hard" or "I'm sorry he's having such a rough time" can affirm parents' feelings, letting them know that you are sharing their sorrow.
- *Resist the urge to make it better.* We desperately want to extinguish hurt in these situations. However, we can unknowingly offer false hope with our words. One mom recently told me that a well-meaning friend, upon learning her son's diagnosis, said, "Oh, that kind of cancer is no big deal! He'll get over it quick!" The speaker meant no harm, of course. However, the mom felt dismissed and silenced.
- *Share success with caution.* When Katie's daughter was ill, she was desperate for happy-ending stories related to her rare disease, and thrilled when the speech pathologist told her that she had seen kids learn to talk again after a stroke. However, she was careful with her words, reminding Katie that every child is

different, and that recovery from brain injury is unpredictable. This helped her form hopeful and realistic expectations.

- *Affirm the parents.* A father recently asked Katie how many second opinions he should seek regarding his daughter's diagnosis. When Katie asked why he asked the question, he said that many folks had insisted he see their doctor or pursue a therapy that was guaranteed to cure. This shook his confidence, even though he trusted the current set of doctors. This dad needed these words of affirmation: "It sounds like you're making great choices, and working with doctors you trust."

Strategy 14—Effective Communication, Part 2 Cinderella's Stepsister

Most of us love fairy tales. They teach some wonderful lessons while entertaining us with princes, clever animals, poisoned apples, and magic kisses. And, of course, everyone loves a happy ending.

Consider Cinderella: The story of a young, left-out girl finding her prince is enchanting. However, Cinderella's stepsisters elicit emotions as well—we sympathize with their humiliating attempts to shove their ungainly, bunion-covered feet into those tiny pumps. But, they also make us angry. How dare they try to push their way into a shoe that was designed uniquely for Cinderella!

What Not to Say

Sometimes, this pushiness occurs outside of fairy tales through flawed communication. Consider the following *Cinderella's stepsister* quotes from teachers and ministry professionals:

- "I used to volunteer for a special needs camp, so I know all about your experiences."
- "You don't need to explain your child's issues. I have three kids of my own."
- "We get it. We've dealt with kids just like yours before. We don't need more information."

Depending on the tone and context in which these statements were delivered, these comments could be construed as comforting to a parent. When a parent has a strong relationship with a teacher or ministry volunteer, these statements may be supportive and encourage peace of mind. However, each of these statements can be a huge roadblock to communication and relationships. When a speaker assumes that he or she knows exactly what a parent is experiencing, communication is abruptly and painfully halted because the speaker is shoving a foot into a shoe that was custom-made for someone else.

Just like Cinderella's custom-made slipper, we are custom-made by God, and so are our children. Our unique personalities and perceptions shape our journeys, and while we may share some common knowledge, it's presumptuous to say we know all about someone's experience. Because we don't.

- *We don't know the shame* that mom felt as she tried to manage her child's outburst in the middle of a first communion service.
- *We don't know the ache* in that dad's heart as he willed his eleven-year-old daughter to write the letters in her name.
- *We don't know the agony* those parents experienced as they watched their child being taken away in handcuffs.

Even if we have experienced those situations, it is important not to diminish the parents' grief and dismiss them by saying, "I know all about that."

What to Say

Instead, offer compassion and mercy through your words:

- "Tell me about what you're experiencing."
- "I can't imagine the ache in your heart."
- "What a terrible thing to happen in your family. I'm so sorry!"

As your conversation continues, try finding solutions:

- "What would make you feel better?"
- "Can I do something that would be helpful? What can I do?"
- "How can we learn more so that church can be a safe and successful place for your family?"

Remember that sometimes, thorough communication has to wait. If a parent is clamoring for your attention on Sunday morning, just as you are ready to preach or teach a lesson, it's okay to make arrangements to talk later. Remember, too, that *you* have unique shoes. Your experiences, talents, and abilities will allow you to support and minister in a way no one else can. Undoubtedly, you will be a tremendous blessing to families as you use these gifts.

Strategy 15—Effective Communication, Part 3
The Assumption-Maker

Communication roadblocks are patterns of behavior during conversations that thwart good, honest communication. So far, we've looked at the minimizer and Cinderella's stepsisters. Next, we'll look at the *assumption-maker*. In this pattern, the listener quickly jumps to conclusions without checking for facts or eliciting more information. When this happens, good conversation is quickly detoured toward defensiveness, with one person trying valiantly—and often angrily—to correct the perceived errors.

Sources of Wrong Assumptions

We've all been guilty of this, haven't we? One wise first-grade teacher started her parent open house night by saying, "Let's make a deal, parents. If you'll believe only half of what your kids say about me, I'll agree to believe only half of what they tell me about you." Everyone chuckled, knowing how easy it is to jump to conclusions based on one statement or observation.

Sometimes, though, assumptions can result in crying rather than laughter. Consider this mother's experience:

> When my daughter came home from school today, she was in tears. She got in the wrong line after recess and was late getting back to her classroom. This kind of thing happens a lot. Ever since she had chemo, she just isn't very organized and gets confused. But the teacher yelled at her and made her sit in the corner while the other kids were having a snack. When I called to talk to the teacher, she cut me off and said, "You know, you've probably bent the rules for Clara since she was in the hospital. She just needs to learn to do what she's told."

The teacher's assumptions caused a setback in the relationship between the parents and the school, as well as embarrassment and lack of confidence for the child.

Consequences of Wrong Assumptions

As we consider how making assumptions causes a breakdown in communication, we need to address the kinds of assumptions that parents make as well. Parents of kids with disabilities often say, "The school just wants to give me as little as possible for my child. It's all about money."

Assumptions affect parents' perceptions of church as well. "The youth team just doesn't get it. I watched a worship service once, so I can tell. They just don't know anything about special needs."

These statements might be based on parents' perceptions of the competence of staff, some of the parents' own experiences, and even what they've been told by others. There might even be some truth in these statements. However, sticking to these, and assuming the worst, breaks down communication and does little to promote collaborative relationships. You can use the suggestions in the sidebar to avoid being an assumption-maker and, instead, foster communications and collaboration.

How to Avoid Being an Assumption-Maker

- *Pray* that your heart, mind, and ears will be open to what the speaker is telling you, and that you can find common ground on which to build cooperation.

- *Make your own opinions* based on your experiences, not those of other staff or parents.

- *Ask questions* to learn the speaker's perspective, and clarify to be sure your perception is accurate: "What I heard you say is . . ." or, "You seem to be telling me that. . .".

- *Extend grace* when others make mistakes. We've become better parents, teachers, and friends because we've shaped our behavior based on what we've learned from some of our errors. We want people to extend grace to us—and we want to do the same.

- *Glorify God* in your conversations.

Strategy 16—Effective Communication, Part 4
The Know-It-All

We've all been at a party with someone who is a know-it-all. They claim mastery in every subject. Sometimes, their ideas and comments can be interesting, but often, their self-proclaimed expertise is exhausting.

The Problem with Know-It-Alls

Parents of kids with disabilities become weary of know-it-alls. As they grasp their child's diagnosis, learn treatment options, and manage behavior, their confidence is often shaken by those who think they know better. In addition, these know-it-all statements quickly halt communication by insinuating that the listener will never master the concept.

- Oh, you don't understand. You've never led a group trip before.
- Kids with disabilities just need structure.
- Your child clearly needs to see a psychiatrist and start medication.

Before we collectively gasp and cluck our tongues to berate these speakers, let's not be hasty. We've said things like this, haven't we?

When we use statements like these, we accomplish our purpose in the short run: no more talking. However, as the church, we need to be interested in the long run. We have a long-term responsibility to encourage and teach each other, and know-it-all communication just doesn't work.

How to Address the Know-It-All Problem

So, how do we address this particular problem? Rather than using your expertise to bully the listener, take a deep breath. Reflect back what you are hearing, and offer your insight—assertively, but kindly. Instead of saying, "You don't understand" or, "you've never led a group trip," try this:

> "It sounds like you would like us to do some social skills training while we're on the trip. That's really important to your child's progress in school and in youth club. What I know to be true is that our travel time and project time on the trip is very unpredictable, and I know I won't be able to follow the script. However, I can be sure that your child is paired with Janie, our college volunteer. She has a great rapport with your child, and she has helped him in group discussions for the last semester. Let's brainstorm some other ideas that will help to make this trip meaningful."

This is just an example, of course, and scripted conversations are much easier than in-the-heat-of-the-moment talks. Perhaps that is why God put our tongues so close to our teeth—so we can quickly bite our tongues instead of saying something we might regret.

Sometimes it's best to say, "Let me think about that." Then, allow yourself some time to reflect and formulate a rational and relationship-building response.

Chapter 5

Main Dishes: Teaching the Truths of the Bible

Jolene's father was a meat-and-potatoes man to the max. To him, an evening meal without meat was merely a snack. A supper without potatoes—or in a pinch, rice, noodles, or corn—wasn't much better. Her dad's insistence on meat and potatoes every evening exasperated her mother. But whenever he was asked why every meal had to include that dynamic duo, his reply was always the same. "Without meat and potatoes, I'll be hungry in an hour."

The truths of the Bible are the meat and potatoes of children's ministry. They should be served to children in every program a church offers. When asked why the presentation of biblical truths is the first priority of children's ministry, the answer is always the same: Without a good helping of truth from God's Word, children will go away spiritually hungry.

Our goal in compiling this chapter is to equip you with a variety of delicious ways to prepare and serve biblical truths to kids. This chapter begins with ideas about how planning and attention to seating arrangements ahead of time make biblical truths tastier, and then explains how to state objectives and establish learning routines that prepare kids to digest new scriptural concepts. Because reading God's

Word is a staple on the menu, you'll find ideas for making reading palatable for reluctant readers. Since chewing on biblical truths is essential to good digestion, the chapter offers discussion strategies and ideas for teaching abstract concepts to concrete thinkers. The chapter ends with strategies that help you determine how well every child understood what was presented.

Your goal when sharing biblical truths with children is not to force-feed them. Your goal is to present truth in ways that make it understandable and accessible to them so that the aroma of Christ, combined with the work of the Holy Spirit, opens their hearts to let Him in.

A Mealtime Prayer

Lord, Your Word is food for the soul, and the children I work with are hungry for it. Show me how to prepare and serve it in tantalizing ways they can digest. Open their hearts to receive the food only You can give. Grant me wisdom to present truth in ways that nurture and strengthen them to live for You.

Strategy 1—Planning Matters

Katie once visited a delightful third grade classroom. The teacher was a master at delivering content and helping kids stay engaged with her lesson. She did this in subtle, loving ways, without embarrassing anyone or making anyone feel inadequate. She had templates of notes for some of the students, making it easier for them to follow along. She paired some of the kids, knowing their strengths and needs, and allowed them to help each other. Some of the students had received pre-teaching materials in their folders the week before. Each student participated actively, at his or her own level, and the objectives of the lesson were accomplished.

Katie noticed, while she was observing, a poster at the back of the room that read,

> If you don't have time to do it right,
> you must have time to do it over.

The teacher probably hung that poster at the beginning of the year, in hopes of inspiring her students. She probably read it countless times. But get this: She was living it.

She was encouraging kids to learn the first time, with gentle reminders and careful prompts, knowing that a stray reprimand or a thoughtless remark could ruin a child's day. Or the whole learning experience. She demonstrated an understanding that although planning her own teaching behavior takes extra time and effort, it very likely prevented issues with behavior, frustration and attention.

She was the kind of teacher who knew that the time it would take to do it over would mean more than reteaching content; it would mean repairing a broken spirit. She took the time to do it right.

Strategy 2—Seating Materials: Settling in for the Lesson

Sitting still has long been an ideal in classrooms and churches. We seem to equate the ability to sit still with good behavior. However, we know that many kids simply cannot be still. Issues with sensory processing, attention, and anxiety may prevent them from sitting motionless. When we understand—and *plan*—for this, we not only demonstrate respect and tolerance, we also increase the likelihood that kids will grasp what we are teaching. Churches can choose from many products to create a comfortable classroom that encourages learning.

Wiggle Cushions. Usually made of plastic and filled with air, these cushions can be placed on the floor or on chairs. Kids using them will be able to rock gently as they participate in class. These cushions can also be placed under tables so that kids can use them as a foot fidget.

Exercise Balls. These large rubber balls are not just for the gym anymore. Exercise balls are a great alternative to traditional seating, and allow kids to bounce or rock as they participate in class. This movement can help them to increase attention or keep calm. Some public schools have taken chairs out of the classroom and replaced them with exercise balls, with great success for all students.

Bands on Chairs. Chair bands are another way to provide comfort for busy feet. This is a low-cost solution, and one that is easy to install. Use a length of rubber tubing and tie it to the front two legs of kids' chairs. Students can then place their feet behind the tubing and push forward. This allows them to get some pressure in their legs and fidget as they participate in class.

Visual Boundaries. Sometimes, a visual reminder can be a powerful tool as well. Some kids have difficulty staying in their own space because of their need to fidget and move. This can become stigmatizing. Consider creating a boundary using colorful tape on the floor around a child's chair. Let the child know that he or she can fidget anywhere inside the office you created. This allows movement while providing elbow room for everyone.

Rocking Chairs. Many churches have rocking chairs in the nursery. These can also be helpful in classrooms. Kids with disabilities are often calmed by the motion of rocking. Having a rocking chair or glider in a classroom might allow a child to take a break, calm down and refocus.

The Non-Seating Solution. Sometimes the best chair is no chair at all. Some kids may want to stretch out on the floor while they work on a coloring sheet or listen to a story. Others might want to stand. Our ability to be flexible and allow kids these options can make a big difference that leads to comfort and joy.

Strategy 3—Stating Objectives

Imagine this: You are sitting at your desk, and your boss approaches you, hands you a set of keys and a package and then says, "Please deliver this right away." What questions might come to mind? What is in this package? To whom should I deliver it? What vehicle will I drive? Where am I supposed to go? How will I get there?

Importance of Objectives

This scenario might be an adventure to some, but most of us would feel rather overwhelmed by it. We all like to know where we're going, and how we're going to get there. The same applies to teaching and learning. When we communicate our plans clearly, our students are more likely to pay attention, engage in the lesson, and remember what they have learned. We, as teachers, are likely to be more successful as well. When we know what we want to accomplish with our students, we tend to focus our teaching and activities to meet our goals.

Definition of Goals

These goals, called "objectives" in education, define the outcomes for our learning activities. While we don't want our churches to become like public schools, there is wisdom in defining—and communicating—what we want students to learn. By doing so, we set a purpose for our activities and help students know what to expect. This is particularly important for students with disabilities, as this practice can relieve anxiety and improve kids' ability to follow directions.

Translating Goals into Kid Language

Many children's ministry materials provide learning objectives for teachers at the beginning of the unit or lesson. Translate these into child-friendly language with simple *we will* statements:

- Today, *we will* read a story from the book of Genesis.
- *We will* create a family tree to show all of Jacob's sons.
- *We will* discuss why Joseph's brothers were jealous.

These statements help students know where they're going during the next hour. Objectives can be posted on a whiteboard or chart and read aloud as students settle into teaching time. Again, we don't want to make church just like school. But we do want to borrow this best practice to enhance learning. After all, the information kids receive at church has eternal significance.

Learning to read is a rite of passage in elementary school; it's also a complicated process. For students with language-based learning disabilities, fluent reading can be an elusive skill, and a source of frustration and embarrassment. In these four strategies, we'll discuss why reading can be challenging for some students and explore options for making kids feel successful and relaxed about reading God's Word.

Strategy 4—Reading Strategies, Part 1
Understanding Reading Disabilities

Parents and Sunday school teachers alike want kids to read and love God's Word. We all agree that reading Scripture is a primary means of spiritual growth. However, for students with reading or language-based learning disabilities, reading a grown up book like the Bible evokes fear, panic, and frustration. In addition, kids may think they aren't good Christians because they can't read Scripture. By understanding reading difficulties and employing some strategies in our classrooms and at home, we can help these students overcome their fear of the Bible.

Dyslexia and Decoding

Competent readers are able to decode—or sound out—unfamiliar words, read fluently, and understand what they have read. They also have well-developed vocabularies, and can monitor their own reading, adjusting their reading rate to enhance comprehension. In contrast, students with reading disabilities have poor decoding skills. Their reading rate is often slow and labored, making comprehension difficult. These students sometimes have difficulty with oral language as well, and struggle to find the right words or retrieve information quickly.

Dyslexia and Memory

Many times, when we think of dyslexia, we assume that kids with this disorder read and write backwards. Although their written work may contain reversed letters and numbers, the backward theory is untrue. However, students with dyslexia have poor memory for symbols and their ability to interpret them rapidly is affected. They need specialized instruction to master these skills. It is important to note that dyslexia is not caused by low intelligence or lack of motivation. Research tells us that the brains of students with learning disabilities process language differently. We also know that as many as one in five students exhibits difficulty with reading tasks.

Solutions for Stress-Free Reading

- **Offer choices.** "I need helpers today. Would you like to read aloud, or would you rather help with the story board?" This allows kids to pass on oral reading without embarrassment.

- **Allow kids to fill in key words as you read.** When reading familiar stories, leave out a word at the end of a sentence and ask kids to fill in the missing word. This helps them to maintain attention and listen for meaning while not requiring them to decode unfamiliar words.

- **Use a story time approach.** Listening to a story can be a nurturing and relaxing experience. Even adults love it. Let your students know that you will handle the reading so they can enjoy God's Word.

- **Create options.** When working with students who have a range of reading ability, create a corner in your room that includes books at multiple reading levels. That way, every child can find a book that is just right.

Dyslexia and Self-Esteem

Perhaps the most concerning aspect of dyslexia is poor self-esteem. Reading and writing are critically important to academic success. Students who have dyslexia may believe that they are incapable of learning. Sometimes, they are the target of teasing and name-calling. Their disability can become a source of shame and anxiety as they struggle to keep pace in the classroom. Approximately one-third of students with dyslexia also have Attention Deficit Hyperactivity Disorders (ADHD), compounding their difficulty and reinforcing their feelings of inadequacy.

As parents and church volunteers, most of us are not trained to remediate these disabilities. However, we can make reading the Bible and participating in church a positive experience. In the following three menu items, we'll discuss some easy-to-use strategies that can help all kids feel successful with their Bibles, so they learn God's Word not just by reading, but by heart.

Strategy 5—Reading Strategies, Part 2
Choral Reading

We have all experienced the discomfort of having to read Scripture aloud. We know how it feels to secretly count ahead in the passage, previewing the words in our verse to be sure that we won't stumble over names or places with odd pronunciations. It can be terrifying, even for the most seasoned, confident reader. Imagine, then, if you were a child with a learning disability for whom a page of text appears jumbled and overwhelming.

Fortunately, many strategies exist to remedy this so that all kids can feel comfortable participating in Scripture reading. In fact, you're probably using lots of these techniques already. These strategies can definitely enhance a child's reading ability and are likely to encourage struggling readers, but they will not cure dyslexia. One of these strategies is choral reading.

What Is Choral Reading?

Choral reading is a solid technique for helping students confidently read Scripture. To understand this method, let's reflect a bit on Katie's first grade Sunday school class. Mrs. Tunder, with her Sunday blue-grey suit, red lipstick, and tightly permed grey curls, taught first grade Sunday school from the beginning of time. And she was good at it. Mothers of wiggly boys loved her structure and her firm but kind style.

Every class period started in the same way: Katie and her classmates read John 3:16 and also a statement of their beliefs: *The Bible is the Word of God.* Mrs. Tunder pointed to each word as the children read. By the end of the year, the first graders had memorized the words on the charts—and had started recognizing them in other places, too. Mrs. Tunder really set her students up for success with this routine.

Benefits of Choral Reading

God's Word, spoken by a group, is powerful and fortifying. In addition, choral reading allows kids to attempt reading unfamiliar words in a nonthreatening, low-risk environment. Repeated choral readings allow kids to increase their fluency in reading Scripture, and also enhance memorization. This can build confidence and improve a child's willingness to continue trying to read the Bible.

How to Facilitate Choral Reading

When introducing choral reading, these steps can help facilitate the process:

1. *Show the students where the passage or verse is located in the Bible.* We want kids to make the connection that what they are about to read is really God's Word, and can be found in any Bible.
2. *Show the same verse or passage to the students on a whiteboard or chart paper.* Verses or passages can also be typed into a PowerPoint slide and projected on a screen. It's important to remember that large passages are visually confusing for kids with dyslexia; showing the passage in smaller segments makes the reading more manageable.
3. *Read the passage aloud to the students, and then invite students to read along.* As the students read together, point to the words in a fluid motion. This helps with fluency, and eliminates the worry children might have about losing their place in the passage.
4. *If time permits, the class should repeat the passage as a group two, or even three, times.* We know that repeated readings allow kids to increase confidence and improve comprehension—very important aspects of reading Scripture. Students are also more likely to pay attention to text when they know what to expect and are able to participate.

At http://netministries.org/Bbasics/bwords.htm, Net Ministries provides an online Bible Pronunciation Guide. The guide contains names and other words that can stump most of us while reading. In addition to a written phonetic pronunciation, an audio version is also available. Even if your Sunday school classroom doesn't have computers and Internet access, it's a worthwhile tool to share with parents and kids.

How to Model Choral Reading

As you read with your students, modeling that reading Scripture is difficult even for adults can be very reassuring to the kids. When they see you struggle with names like Methuselah or Elimelech, they may feel more confident as they try new words themselves.

It's also important to model strategies for decoding these unfamiliar words. For example, when reading the word "frankincense" a teacher might say, "Hmmm. This word is really long and looks difficult. Let's see. I could take this word apart. 'Frank' is a name I know. The next part of the word is 'in' and I know that word too."

You might also suggest asking a friend or skipping the word and going back to it later, or substituting another word that might make sense. These are all appropriate strategies for reading that will minimize frustration.

Strategy 6—Reading Strategies, Part 3 Products to Enhance Reading

We all agree that reading Scripture is an important part of spiritual growth. In the last piece, we discussed ways to encourage fluent reading through choral reading activities and teacher-led reading. Below, you'll find a list of ideas and products to try in your classrooms to make Scripture reading kid-friendly and stress-free.

Music Resources

Teach raps or rhymes that help kids remember the books of the Bible in order. The *Wee Sing Bible Songs* book and CD have songs for Old and New Testament books. It also has a rap for helping kids remember the twelve disciples' names. Songs and rhymes are a great way for kids to learn their way around the Bible. In addition, a group song or chant is a wonderful way to regain kids' attention or to help them transition to a new activity.

> *Use a group song or chant to transition from one activity to the next by saying something like, "As we move to the craft table, let's sing the Old Testament books."*

Bible Tab Resources

Upper elementary kids, middle and high schoolers will benefit from Bible tabs to help them find books of the Bible more easily. They can be color-coded in addition to using the names of the books to allow for greater speed and accuracy. For example, you might say, "Please turn to Luke chapter 2. Luke is a gospel, so it will be in the green tabs on your Bible."

Bible tabs can be made as a class activity. Post-It™ has tabs that can easily be used for this purpose. If you choose to do this, it's important to remember that the tabs are small, which can frustrate kids with fine motor problems as they attempt to write on the labels. Another solution is Kids Horizontal Bible Tabs. These are divided into categories and also have graphics for each book of the Bible; this will make locating books easy for kids who struggle with reading.

Overlay and Highlighter Resources

For some students, the visual confusion of text makes reading overwhelming and frustrating. In addition, the glare of the white page can irritate some readers. Many times, students with reading difficulties also have attention problems that interfere with fluent, focused reading. To minimize this, students can use color overlays. These softly colored, transparent plastic overlays highlight text to facilitate reading and focus. In addition, removable highlighter tape can assist students with locating a specific word or verse. When trying these materials, it will be helpful to allow all students to have a turn using them; this avoids students feeling both left out or singled out.

Resources:

- IRLEN Colored Overlays for Reading: http://www.amazon.com/IRLEN-Colored-Overlays-Reading-Sample/dp/B003LNMHTU
- Highlighter Strips: http://www.enasco.com/c/reading/Teacher+Resources/Highlighter+Strips/?ref=breadcrumb
- Kid's Horizontal Bible Tabs: http://www.christianbook.com/kids-horizontal-bible-tabs/pd/105080
- Post-It Tabs: http://www.post-it.com/wps/portal/3M/en_US/PostItNA/Home/Products/~/Post-it/Tabs/?N=5927572+4327&rt=r3
- Wee Sing Bible Songs: http://weesing.com/Books-Music/Wee-Sing-Bible-Songs

Strategy 7—Reading Strategies, Part 4
Reading Practice Makes Perfect Participation

What's the buzz in churches a month or two before Christmas? Christmas pageant practice, of course. Kids work on their parts at home. Entire Sunday school hours are devoted to rehearsal. Saturday mornings are commandeered, too. And what's the result of all that practice? The pageant goes off, not without a hitch, but with every child participating and hearing applause at the end. What made it happen? Practice!

Practice for Participation

The strategy that makes it possible for every child to participate in church pageants—practice—can also make it possible for every child to read aloud at Sunday school, midweek programs, and other children's church programs. And because reading a few sentences is much less complicated than staging a church pageant, practice doesn't require the entire Sunday school hour or any Saturday mornings.

Practice Preparation

The preparations for practice are quite simple and well worth a little extra time, as the planning will reap benefits.

Choose a passage. The passage could be from the Bible, a story printed in the Sunday school paper, a skit, or other material to be read aloud.

Divide it into sections. Have at least one section per child. Go ahead and pencil names in the teacher's manual—that's what it's for, after all—to avoid confusion later on.

Assign a passage to each child. Choose shorter passages with easier vocabulary for struggling readers. The title of the story or one sentence may be enough for some children. Save the longer passages for fluent readers. The kids will know what's going on, but if they've been informed about the special needs of peers, they will be accommodating. (See *The Power of Story in Explaining Special Needs*, page 67.)

Practice Reading Together

With those preparations in place, it's time to teach kids the process of reading practice. Once again, the process is simple.

Assign each child a passage. Let them pencil a circle around their parts or lightly pencil mark the beginning and end of their parts in the Bible. Contrary to what book lovers say, the sky will not fall when kids write in a book. However, the tiny visual cues may cause a child's stress level to drop measurably.

Explain how to practice. Tell the children that on the count of three, they will all practice their passage out loud at the same time for five minutes. (Close the door before starting to count. This gets noisy.) Then set a timer for five minutes, count *1...2...3* and let them start.

Listen in. While the children are practicing, walk around and kneel beside struggling readers. Read with them until you're sure they can read their parts well. If the class has more than one struggling reader, have volunteers or buddies do the same with them.

Read aloud. When the timer rings, stop the practice and have the children read their passages one by one. And try not to cry when some kids read aloud with confidence for the first time in their lives.

Applaud. Yeah. After everybody's done reading, go ahead and do it. Why save the applause for just the Christmas pageant?

Reading Practice Modifications

Consider implementing these reading practice modifications for children with special needs:

- Let kids with auditory sensitivities wear noise-dampening headphones during the practice time.

- Pair a child who is easily distracted with a buddy. Have the buddy take the child to a quiet place to practice.

- Offer a copy of the passage for families to take home if students would like to practice during the week.

Strategy 8—Imagination Unleashed: Role Play

Role playing is imprinted on the DNA of young children. Their free time is spent playing house, school, astronaut, hairdresser, race car driver, restaurant, firefighter, and whatever else captures their imagination. When church ministry volunteers allow kids to act out scenarios as part of church activities, they tap into role play DNA.

Six Reasons Role Play Is Good for Kids

Role playing is like apples. Kids like them and they're good for kids for many reasons. Here are a few:

- It lets kids get up and move.
- It encourages empathy by allowing kids to walk in someone else's shoes.
- It gives them a way to practice social skills.
- It gives them a chance to practice the content presented.

- It makes Bible stories come alive.
- It's fun.

Now, think back to why you liked to pretend when you were a kid and add your reasons to the list.

Set the Stage for Role Play

The older kids get, the more they need to feel accepted and secure before they will participate in role play. To set the stage for acceptance and security, get to know the kids you are working with. Which ones like the limelight? Who are the leaders? Before introducing the first role play, ask the kids identified by your answers to participate. Offer to practice with them, so they are comfortable. Another way to build interest is to role play a story for the class. Then ask a volunteer to act out another scene with you. And always, always, always give kids the option to pass.

Ways to Role Play

Role play can be organized differently, depending on the children's developmental age, comfort level, and skills. For children not able to read, allowing them to dress up in costumes and play with props is a good place to start. Then, ask them to act out a story while you read it aloud. Once kids can read, they can dabble in role play by sitting around a table to read a short script. From there, they can move on to standing up and acting it out. Add props and costumes if the kids are agreeable. Or ask a child to be interviewed as a character from a Bible story.

If coaching or modifications are required so a child with special needs can participate, do what needs to be done. Feed lines. Pair kids to play one part together. Practice a time or two. But, if role play pushes some children beyond their comfort zone, don't force the issue. Instead, allow them to be the audience. Show them how to cheer on the heroes and applaud at the end. Who knows, once they're hooked on audience participation, they might feel accepted and secure enough to join the action on stage, too.

Free Skits for Role Playing

Several websites post free children's ministry skits for role playing. Here are a few to get you started:

- http://www.kidssundayschool.com/14/gradeschool/skits.php
- http://www.kidssundayschool.com/14/gradeschool/skits.php?start=m&end=n

Strategy 9—Questioning Strategies

Children, even the most shy and noncommunicative ones, want their voices to be heard. At the same time, they have no desire to participate in group discussions until they are convinced their environment is a safe and positive place. Even when they do feel emotionally safe, they may refrain from speaking because they fear giving a wrong answer. Like a skilled dinner host, you can employ questioning strategies designed to draw out children so their voices are heard and appreciated.

Why to Use Questioning Strategies

Questioning strategies serve several purposes that can benefit all children and accommodate the needs of kids with disabilities. Here are several reasons to ask kids questions during church activities:

To stimulate discussion. Some kids love to answer questions, whether or not they know the answer. And since kids know that at church God, Jesus, or the Bible are the correct answers in most cases, they're willing to give it a shot. But good questions focus the discussion so more kids are willing to participate.

To elicit information. Kids who attend church activities may have heard Bible stories more than once. Good questions reveal what kids know or don't know and what misconceptions they have. Then the leader can determine what to review briefly and what to emphasize during the lesson.

To engage every child. Thoughtfully crafted questions are a way to engage every child in the room. Children with a basic understanding can be asked yes/no questions, or ones dealing with simple facts. Ask those with a greater grasp of the discussion topic application questions about how the story or lesson relates to real life. Ask kids ready for a challenge to compare and contrast, give opinions, make judgments, or create something new. Check the sidebar below for examples of each kind of question.

To guide children to the answer. Guiding children to the right answer is akin to a fishing expedition. Experienced fishermen know how to teach newcomers to cast the line over and over with increasing accuracy until they discover the location of the fish. In the same way, increasingly specific questions can guide kids to the answer as they experience the joy of discovery.

To stimulate a child's thinking. Children who are encouraged to consider and answer questions find stimulation to ask their own questions. Kids who ask questions are curious and engage in problem-solving more often, too.

How to Use Questioning Strategies

Questioning strategies are a crucial component of learning. That's why education departments of colleges and universities offer classes on the subject. But many questioning strategies are easy to use, and several of them are briefly described below.

- *Ask open-ended questions.* To stimulate discussion participation, ask questions that require more than a yes or no answer. Instead of asking, "Did you have a good week?" ask, "What happened to you this week?" Replace "Did Jesus like little children?" with "How did Jesus treat children?" Rather than, "Was Jonah in the belly of a whale? try this: "Why was Jonah in the belly of a whale?"
- *Modify questions based on ability.* Yes/no or short answer questions may be appropriate for a child who has speech delays or uses a word board to communicate. Short questions may also be enough for children attending for the first time. Once children become more at ease and their knowledge base grows, move on to more open-ended questions.

Questions to Engage Every Child

This chart gives examples of questions from the basic level to more complex.

Knowledge:	Who did Daniel work for?
	Where was Jesus born?
Comprehension:	Describe what it was like for Daniel to work in Babylon.
	Why was Jesus born in a stable?
Application:	Can you act out the conversation between Daniel and the king?
	How do you think people might treat a family as poor as Joseph and Mary's?
Analysis:	Would you compare what happened in the lion's den to what happened in the fiery furnace?
	Why do you think the shepherds and Herod reacted so differently?
Evaluation:	Why do you think Daniel wouldn't worship the king?
	Why do you think God allowed Jesus to be born in a manger?

- *Rephrase questions from open-ended to specific.* Use this strategy after asking an open-ended question that receives nothing but blank stares that say, "We have no idea what you're talking about. No way will we try to answer and make fools of ourselves." Faced with those stares, pose a less difficult question that contains tidbits of information as hints. If the question "Why did baby Jesus come to earth at Christmas?" falls flat, follow up with "Who loves you so much that He sent Jesus to earth at Christmas?" Or perhaps, "How much do you think God loved us to send His Son to earth?"
- *Prearrange questions for specific children.* Talk with a hesitant child before class about the question you will be asking him. Go over the answer together, so the child can answer confidently. This strategy gives the child a chance to get used to speaking in front of peers. Parents can also be notified ahead of time to practice with the child.
- *Model thinking aloud to children.* When adults think out loud, they show children how it's done. So while reading a story, stop before turning the page and say, "I wonder what will happen to Daniel next. Hmm. He already stood up to the king's decree once. I think he'll do it again. Now I'll turn the page and see."

When these strategies are employed in a positive and inclusive environment, kids will begin to engage in discussions. It may take some time, but eventually everyone's voice will be valued and heard.

Strategy 10—"Every Pupil Response" Strategies

We've all experienced the feelings of uncertainty and nervousness when we attempt to share our ideas with unfamiliar folks. Kids experience this, too. Those with disabilities may experience roadblocks when trying to merge onto the discussion highway. This difficulty can stem from a variety of causes, such as anxiety, language-based learning disabilities, memory issues, and motor-based problems like apraxia. Whatever the reason, teachers and volunteers can help kids participate comfortably by trying some of the strategies below.

Offer Choices
Sometimes, emotional or learning problems prevent kids from answering a question with confidence. To remedy this, offer the needed

words in the body of the question. For example: "Joe, for our class service project, should we make a bulletin board or clean the toy room?"

Joe can voice his opinion without having to formulate a whole sentence. Similarly, yes/no questions can allow a quieter member of the class to participate verbally, or even through a nod or shake of the head.

Every Pupil Response

We've all led discussions during which a few kids do the majority of the talking. When this happens, it's hard to assess whether everyone has mastered the content, and even more difficult to encourage some of the less verbal kids to participate. Instead of asking, "Who can tell me if Jonah was obedient?" try saying, "If you think Jonah was obedient, give me a thumbs up; if you think he was disobedient, give me a thumbs down." Once the kids show their opinions, you can ask Jane, "why do you think that?" or "Mike, give me an example that helped you form your opinion."

This strategy allows students to show what they know without the risk of being put on the spot. The added benefit is increased attention for all kids because they know that the teacher is expecting a response from everyone. To keep kids even more engaged, teachers can change the response method. Instead of thumbs up/thumbs down, use a variety of prompts: hands on head, finger on ear, hand on heart, and so on.

Stage a Set-Up

Kids who have difficulty with conversation sometimes do better with a bit of preparation. Covertly pulling children aside and letting them know the questions that will be asked during discussion allows them time to ready themselves for participation.

Think-Pair-Share

Sometimes, it is easier for a student to share ideas with one person than with a whole group. When asking an open-ended question like "How can you show that you love your neighbor?" try the think-pair-share strategy:

- First, tell students that you are going to ask a question, and you would like them to think quietly about their answer.
- Next, ask students to tell their ideas to one peer in the group.
- Finally, ask the students to have one member of the pair tell the ideas.

This allows kids to participate in a structured social activity which may be less threatening than jumping into a large-group discussion.

Popsicle Picks

When we ask a question, some students can quickly monopolize the conversation. One strategy that can add some structure is eliminating the hand-raising in favor of picking a name at random. Sheri Halagan, a National Board Certified teacher, writes each student's name on a popsicle stick and then picks a name to answer her questions. Lest you think that this might put a shy student on the spot, Sheri is quite savvy when randomly selecting names. Although the students believe that she is choosing names randomly, Sheri knows her students and their needs. She carefully matches kids and questions to set everyone up for success during group discussions.

Wait-Time

We are all uncomfortable with awkward pauses in conversations. However, as teachers, we need to embrace the silence. In an age of instant gratification, we need to remember—and teach children—that sometimes, we need to think things through, gather our thoughts, and consider the possibilities. It's necessary to build some wait-time into discussions with kids: "I'm going to describe a problem in our community, and I want everyone to just think about what your solution to this problem might be." This wait-time helps every student. In addition, when calling on students individually, resist moving on too quickly when the student doesn't answer. Allowing wait-time can offer an opportunity for a child to be heard.

Strategy 11—Group Discussion Strategies

Oh! Oh! I know! I know the answer! Call on me!

It's hard to ignore the enthusiasm of a student who is eager to share ideas. However, group discussions can be difficult for some students with hidden disabilities. These kids might struggle with turn-taking, reading social cues, impulse control and short-term memory. As a result, their contributions to conversations can be off-topic or repetitive. When called on, they may monologue about a topic of interest, or struggle to retrieve the words and phrases necessary to answer the question. Sound familiar? If so, here are a couple of real-life scenarios, along with solutions that really work.

Scenario 1

Problem: A kindergarten student with autism who loves raising his hand during Sunday school discussions became frustrated and angry when he wasn't called on each time. This frustration often led to tears, and sometimes even tantrums. His volunteer buddy tried to distract him and help him to take turns, but he continued to struggle.

Solution: We suggested that the buddy give this child two or three Legos. Each Lego represented one turn in the group conversation. After each turn, the child gave a Lego to his buddy. When the Legos were gone, he was done with his turns for that conversation.

The Result: The student did very well with this tangible reminder of turn-taking. He was able to share ideas with increased structure and remained in his class for the entire hour.

Scenario 2

Problem: When participating in a girls' small group, a ninth grade student with ADHD blurted her opinion to every discussion question before the other girls had an opportunity to speak. The youth group leader noticed that some girls in the group had started to roll their eyes and tune this student out.

Solution: The leader took the student aside and gently talked with her about the issue. The leader suggested that the student try being the third or fourth person to answer a question instead of the first. They also developed a nonverbal cueing system that helped the student manage the length of her responses.

The Result: More aware of her tendency to blurt out answers, the student used her new strategy in youth group with great success. She also applied it to school discussions and informal conversations with friends.

Strategy 12—Teaching Abstract Concepts to Concrete Thinkers

The purpose of children's ministry is to introduce kids to Jesus so they can know His love and compassion and become part of His family. Kids on the autism spectrum, or who have processing disorders, or who live with developmental delays often flounder when presented with abstract spiritual concepts they can't comprehend. So how can we communicate abstract spiritual truths that define the Christian faith to kids who are concrete thinkers?

Kids Are Concrete Thinkers

An understanding of the difference between concrete and abstract thinkers is a good place to begin. The sidebar provides some examples. Also remember this rule of thumb: The younger the children, the more concrete their thinking will be. Typically developing kids between the ages of two and seven are very concrete thinkers, while those between the ages of seven and twelve begin to think logically and apply reason to concrete events. Only from the ages of twelve and up does abstract thought appear in typically developing children. And the thinking skills of kids with special needs often mature more slowly.

Concrete versus Abstract Thinkers

Concrete Thinkers	Abstract Thinkers
Count items.	Think about numbers.
Know that Sam likes Jill.	Reflect on emotions like affection.
Think story is about not stealing.	Think story is about resisting sin to honor Christ.
Apply logic to one problem.	Generalize logical thinking from one problem to another.
Think *Go take a hike* means that.	Think *Go take a hike* means *Please leave.*

Tips for Teaching Concrete Learners

Does that mean the vast majority of kids in children's ministry programs think at a concrete level? It certainly does. And it also means that the following tips for teaching concrete learners will benefit every child in the program.

Eliminate sarcasm. Sarcasm requires abstract thinking skills to determine what the speaker really means. So get rid of it.

Avoid Christian jargon. Concrete thinkers won't process the phrases "Ask Jesus into your heart," or "Washed in the blood of the Lamb" the way an adult believer will. They'll be too worried about how Jesus can fit in their hearts and how to wash off the sheep blood to consider a relationship with Christ.

Limit theological concepts. Again, kids under the age of twelve aren't ready for theological concepts like propitiation, justification, sanctification, regeneration; limit time spent on those big ideas. If a particularly advanced thinker in your class asks about them, affirm the child's enthusiasm for delving into these concepts, and extend an invitation to discuss it further when you can provide some individual attention.

Think before you answer. When a child asks a question requiring an abstract answer, think about how to respond. Usually, kids want simple answers, not theological ones. So ask a few probing questions to determine what the child really wants to know. Then give a brief answer using kid-friendly language.

Give concrete examples and use concrete language. Kids understand concrete examples. So anchor faith concepts with examples of real people, from the Bible and throughout history, who demonstrated them. Use vocabulary familiar to kids. If they appear puzzled, ask questions to check for understanding, and reword if necessary.

Remember, God gave us the perfect example of how to explain an abstract concept to concrete minds. He sent Jesus, a concrete person with a real life anchored in time and space, so we can draw close to the invisible God. Our job in children's ministry is to follow that example and share Jesus so that children of all ages and stages want to come to Him.

Chapter 6

Side Dishes:
Activities to Enhance Learning

Good cooks and dinner party hosts know something Jolene's father frequently overlooked: meat and potatoes alone make a heavy meal. A well-balanced meal includes side dishes featuring lighter fare. Complementary flavors makes diners leave the table satisfied rather than weighed down. Diners who leave the party savoring a delectable mix of tastes and textures will be eager to enjoy another meal there soon.

In much the same way, we need to remember that balance is important. Yes, the truth of the Bible will always be the center of children's ministry. But special needs ministry leaders acknowledge that those truths are enhanced when served with side dishes that bring out subtle flavors and are more palatable for those who enjoy more varied fare. This chapter contains side-dish recipes designed to complement the strategies for presenting biblical truths in chapter 5. It serves up handy-dandy resources and strategies to help kids settle down and increase their ability to pay attention.

Biblical truth remains at the center of special needs ministry. But as Christ himself showed on numerous occasions, side dishes have a place at the table, too. A piece of bread tastes good with fish. Bread dipped in wine rounds out even the most solemn meal. Should we settle for anything less?

A Prayer for Balance

Lord Jesus, You are the God of perfect balance. You know when we need heavy truth and when we benefit from something lighter. Show me how to bring balance into these lessons and activities. Open my eyes to side-dish ideas that will help the children in my care better comprehend truth from Your Word.

Strategy 1—Fidget Toys and Tools

When we offer training to teachers and volunteers, we're often asked if fidget toys, like stress balls and tangles, really work to help students focus and manage behavior. Our answer? Yes. And no. Some days, beautifully. Other days? Not so much. Certain kids? You bet. Others? Hardly ever. Helpful, aren't we?

Why Fidget Toys Work Sometimes and Not Others

Special education professionals agree that the effectiveness of fidget toys largely depends on the needs of the child. While fidgets are a popular recommendation at IEP planning meetings and workshops, they are not a cure-all. Sheri Halagan comments, "I wish they were the answer for every child. They're not." Intervention specialist Amy Belew, also a National Board Certified teacher, agrees: "They become a distraction for so many kids."

Teachers and volunteers wonder, then, why fidget toys work like magic for some kids, but not others. Child psychologist Dr. Sherri McClurg explains that this is based on the strengths and needs of the child. "Fidgets are great for kids with anxiety or spectrum disorders; kids with ADHD will struggle to use them." She then explains that fidget toys may fill a sensory need for students on the spectrum, and also can reduce tension and nervousness in kids who struggle with anxiety. Students with ADHD, however, may become focused on the fidget toy to the exclusion of the class discussion or activity.

How to Use Fidget Toys Effectively

Unfortunately, many volunteers and pastors don't have the luxury of knowing students' diagnoses in order to apply a diagnostic and prescriptive approach to intervention. So, then, what can the church folks do to help all students in a classroom pay attention and participate effectively?

- *Be a good student of your students.* Observe them carefully and decide what strategies might be appropriate based on what you see and hear.
- *Teach them how to fidget.* "Kids don't know as much as we think they know about how to act in the classroom," Halagan shares. Before handing out fidget toys, she advises, teachers should demonstrate their use and allow kids to practice. Later, if a student's fidget toy is becoming a distraction—the stress ball is being thrown at a target across the room—Halagan recommends verbally cueing the child: "Show me how to use that in our class." This kind of prompt allows the child to remember the rules and practice them.
- *Set limits.* If the misuse of the fidget toy continues, Halagan says it's okay to take the toy away with the assurance: "We'll try this again next time."
- *Look at yourself.* Dr. Rachel Jones, an elementary school principal remarks, "Instead of scrutinizing their behavior, change yours." If students consistently struggle with inattention, teachers should take a look at the pace and content of lessons, the classroom environment and arrangement, and their own interactions with students. Often, changes in teacher behavior can yield great increases in students' participation and attention.

So, what's the bottom line? Fidget toys do work, but they're not a panacea. That's something to celebrate, because every child is a unique and fabulous creation.

Check out Katie's favorite online source for fidget toys: www.therapyshoppe.com

Strategy 2—Visual Timers

We are all in a hurry these days, and sometimes it is very hard to keep track of the time. Monitoring time can be especially difficult for children and adults with ADHD, autism spectrum disorders, and learning disabilities.

The concept of time is abstract; calculating elapsed time or estimating how long a task might take can be extremely difficult. Students can become confused by phrases such as "quarter after" or "five to." The increased use of digital clocks makes learning analog clocks difficult, especially when we consider the fractional elements of time such as the half hour.

A visual timer can be a very helpful tool to assist students with these issues. The timer can be set for a length of time which becomes highlighted in red. Students can then see the time elapsing as the red color disappears minute by minute. This helps students understand and manage time visually.

> Learn more about visual timers at http://www.timetimer.com/. Be sure to read about visual timer watches, as well as applications for computers, iPhones and iPods.

Students with autism particularly respond to this, as they function well with visual cues. For students who are anxious, this can be a comforting tool. For example, a teacher can tell a student, "When the red time is gone, it will be time to find your mom in the lobby." This helps the student see that the separation from parents is temporary.

Strategy 3—Social Stories

Before driving to a new destination, Jolene prints out the directions and a map. Then she traces the route with a finger while muttering *Okay, this is the first turn, then ten miles until the interstate,* and so on. What is she doing? Creating a social story for the trip.

Social stories, sometimes referred to as behavioral stories or scripted stories, are used to teach children on the autism spectrum about social cues, the feelings of others, and appropriate responses. They can be an effective special needs ministry tool.

What Are Social Stories?

Social stories are short stories about common social situations encountered by children. Each story is written from the child's point of view and is illustrated with clip art, or photographs of the child engaged in the situation or activity. Before the child engages in the activity, he reads through the story, or has it read to him.

How Can Social Stories Be Used at Church?

Social stories are used in three main ways: to prepare for a new event or experience like moving to a new Sunday school class, to teach a positive behavior such as waiting in line at the drinking fountain, or to teach a new skill such as cleaning up the craft table. Within those three categories, possible social story topics abound.

How Is a Social Story Written?

Social stories contain four kinds of sentences. Descriptive sentences tell where the activity takes place, who's involved, what each person is doing, and why they are doing it. Perspective sentences relate the emotions, thoughts, and reactions of the people involved. Affirmative sentences enhance descriptive and perspective sentences. They may state a value or opinion, stress important points, refer to a rule, or reassure. Directive sentences suggest the desired response, or choice of responses, in positive terms. Most of the sentences should be the first three kinds. Here are other tips for writing effective social stories about children's ministry activities.

- Get input for the story from parents, if possible.
- Write the story from the child's point of view. Use first person language such as, "I say hello to my Sunday school teacher."
- Use positive language. Say what the child should do instead of what they shouldn't do.
- Use language appropriate to the child's developmental level.
- Use visual supports—line drawings, clip art, photographs, or pictures—appropriate to the child's level of development. (See *Visual Schedules*, page 40 for more information.)
- Focus on one new event, behavior, or skill per story.
- Introduce only one story at a time.
- Practice the social story with the child before the challenging situation begins. Remember that the child may need to practice the story several times.
- Share the story with others who work with the child at church (children's ministry leader, coteachers, volunteers, buddies, etc.) so the child gets a consistent message.

Where Can Social Story Resources Be Found?

Tutorials and resources about creating social stories, as well as downloadable examples, abound on the Internet. They can be found by typing "social stories" or "how to create social stories" in a search engine. Here's a list of our favorites:

- Tips for creating social stories: http://www.spectronics.com.au/blog/tools-and-resources/tips-for-creating-successful-social-stories/
- The Watson Institute downloadable behavior stories: www.the-watsoninstitute.org

- Vanderbilt University downloadable scripted stories for social situations: http://csefel.vanderbilt.edu/resources/strategies.html
- Kids Can Dream offers links to social stories from all over the Internet: http://kidscandream.webs.com/page12.htm
- Sensory Processing Disorder Pinterest page: http://www.pinterest.com/sensoryprocessi/social-stories/

Four Kinds of Social Story Sentences

Descriptive: My name is_____. On Wednesday night, I go to Awana at 6:15. Game time gets very noisy.

Perspective: My Sunday school teacher knows lots of Bible stories. Some kids like to sing during group time.

Affirmative: I will keep my lips off the water fountain spout. This keeps germs from spreading. The toilet makes noise when it flushes. That's okay.

Directive: I will ask my buddy to take me to the quiet room when game time is noisy. I will put on headphones during singing time.

Strategy 4—Tally Marks: Positive Feedback... No Assembly Required

Kids live in the moment; for them, waiting five minutes for positive feedback feels like an eternity. They respond much better to immediate feedback, and tally marks are an easy, no-assembly-required means of giving it.

Tally marks are little vertical lines that look like the digit 1. Once four marks have been made close together, the fifth mark, a diagonal one overlaying the other four, bundles them into a neat group of five. Much easier for counting and fascinating to children.

These steps turn those tiny little marks into a positive feedback tool and magical motivator when completing paper and pencil activities.

Introduce tally marks. Ask the kids what they know about tally marks. If needed, fill in any deficits in their understanding, or review the process by demonstrating how to make and count them. Then explain that they will be instructed to put a tally mark at the top of their paper when you see them doing something very good. When they take their papers home, they can show them to their parents and tell them that each tally mark means they did something good. Stars or smiley faces can be used instead if they are better motivators for children.

Practice Tally Marks

Next, if the children exhibited good behavior during your explanation say, "You've all been listening attentively, so put a tally mark on your paper." Or single out one child and say, "Juan, you are sitting so quietly in your chair. Put a tally mark on your paper."

Distribute Tally Marks Freely

Once tally marks have been introduced, distribute them freely for several sessions. Every time you see a child, several children, or everyone doing something right, acknowledge it by distributing tally marks.

Explain the Behavior

Always explain the behavior that earned a tally mark. The explanation praises the recipient and motivates others to demonstrate acceptable behavior. Here are a few examples:

- "Akira, you came in and went right to the puzzle table to help Maria. Put a tally mark on your paper."
- "Albert, you made eye contact while I gave directions. You earned a tally mark."
- "Our group was so quiet moving from large group to our classroom, everyone gets a tally mark."

Give Tally Marks to Kids with Behavior Challenges

Observe children with special behavior challenges, catch them being good, and give them tally marks as often as possible. They may get a bit giddy if they usually don't get much positive feedback. But they'll get used to it.

Eventually, the children will internalize the behaviors the tally marks have been reinforcing, and the use of them will diminish. You can dust them off now and then, when behaviors grow lax and children need some retraining. When that happens, target the behavior to be reinforced and find one child who's demonstrating it. Then announce why he or she has earned a tally mark. Chances are, their behavior will improve, too. When that happens, give tally marks all around. Good for them. Easy for you. And no assembly required.

Strategy 5—Sequencing Cards and Other Strategies for Retelling

Jesus loves me, this I know
For the Bible tells me so.

These words, sung in churches worldwide, communicate an important truth: the Bible is the primary source of information about the love of God through His Son, Jesus.

More than anything, we want kids in our programs to know about Jesus. To accomplish this, we teach Bible stories that will help them understand the history of our faith, the character of God and the men and women who learned to follow His Word.

While we want all kids to internalize these stories, we must remember that comprehension can be very challenging for students with disabilities. Some children lack the ability to remember what they have heard, while others struggle to recall information in an organized way. Others may have difficulty finding the main idea, and others might not be able to retrieve words that describe the sequence of the story. Whatever the difficulty, remembering and retelling a story can be a frustrating experience. Several strategies can be used to support kids as they learn Bible stories. Fortunately, these activities can be used—and enjoyed!—by all kids.

Sequencing Cards. Provide several pictures that depict the beginning, middle and end of the Bible story. Have kids put these in order and then color them. They can use these to retell the story at church and also on the way home.

Felt Boards. A tried and true strategy, felt boards can be as popular with kids now as in the past. Felt characters have a soft and appealing texture as well, making them easy for kids with sensory issues to use.

Puppets. Kids love a puppet show, and many enjoy the chance to perform. Create stick puppets of the characters in a story and allow the children to retell it through a puppet show.

Drama. As with puppets, kids enjoy a good show. Encourage them to act out what they have learned. This can be an effective group strategy, utilizing kids who can remember sequence and details to direct as others act out the story.

Summary Books. Like sequencing cards, these small books help kids retell the story using pictures (or, for kids who can read, words). Once the children get them in order, they can staple them together and illustrate or color them.

Rereading. For some children, hearing a story again and again is comforting and helpful. Don't be afraid to reread and review stories with your students. After all, we want these stories to be remembered in their heads and their hearts.

Strategy 6—First/Then Boards

All kids need structure, and most appreciate knowing what to expect. However, some children with disabilities require additional help with this. The process of hearing directions, beginning and completing a task, and then moving on to the next thing requires a complex set of skills. Kids who have trouble with maintaining attention, organization, or verbal directions might become confused. For those children, a detailed schedule may not be the best solution. Instead, a First/Then board can provide predictability, structure, and a higher level of success.

The First/Then Concept
The First/Then concept is quite easy. Using a chart, whiteboard, or magnet board, provide an icon or picture of a task that must be done first and then the task or reward that follows.

First: Bible story	Then: Computer time
First: Worship time	Then: Craft time
First: Wash hands	Then: Snack time
First: Group time	Then: Choose sticker

Creating a First/Then Board
First/Then pictures can be adhered to the chart with Velcro® or magnets. The charts can be modified to meet the needs of the students as well. Some students may be able to help organize their own schedule, while others will need adult help with this. For kids who need frequent reinforcement, a menu of options can be offered, and the children can choose what reward appeals to them.

Items to use as reinforcers:
1. Stickers
2. Small candies
3. Computer time
4. Game time
5. Small tokens or prizes

First/Then Variations

If a child benefits from a First/Then type of schedule, teachers can prepare laminated cards that are held together with a staple or vocabulary ring. After each task, kids can turn the page to see what is next.

The preparation for this type of schedule can be time-consuming initially. However, once the materials are made, they can be used with other students during weekday programs such as Awana or Pioneer Clubs.

Strategy 7—Reteaching Strategies

All children can learn, given enough time.

This wise maxim can change a person's perspective about the importance of reteaching gospel truths to children with learning delays and other special needs. Because if it's true—all children can learn, given enough time—then reteaching becomes a way to work with the Holy Spirit to implant the good news of the gospel into young hearts. And here's more good news about reteaching the good news: It can be oodles of fun.

Reteaching ≠ Repeating the Same Lesson the Same Way

Effective reteaching is more than repeating the same lesson in the same way. Traditional teaching methods work best for children who have strong visual or auditory skills. In other words, they can easily learn by hearing or seeing information and then talking about it. But children with special needs often learn differently from their typically developing peers. They learn best by doing, by feeling, or perhaps by listening to music. Therefore, effective reteaching means presenting concepts in a different way.

Not every concept bears reteaching. But if responses to discussion questions (see *Questioning Strategies*, page 90) indicate misconceptions about basic biblical truths, then reteaching is in order.

Reteaching = Interactive Fun

Because many kids learn best by doing, reteaching is an opportunity for interactive fun. Here are a few ideas to get those creative juices flowing:

- *Use music.* When information enters the brain set to music, it can be recalled decades later. So bring in a kids' praise CD about the concept or Bible story being taught. Encourage kids to sing along. Add motions. Dance along.
- *Write a song.* Take a familiar melody, such as "Twinkle, Twinkle Little Star" or "Three Blind Mice." Work together to write a song.

- *Add rhythm.* Add rhythm and a beat to make it easier to memorize a Bible verse.
- *March around.* March around to the beat while reciting the verse several times.
- *Draw pictures.* Retell a story and draw pictures on the whiteboard during the telling. Stick people are perfectly acceptable. Then erase the board and have kids draw the pictures as the story is read again.
- *Play a game.* Depending on what's being retaught, the age of children, and their developmental level, modified versions of *Password, Concentration, Pictionary, Who Wants to Be a Millionaire,* or *Jeopardy* can work well.
- *Act it out.* Have kids act out the story as you read it. Or use a skit that's already been written. (See *Role Playing*, page 88.)
- *Know/Wonder/Learn (KWL).* Create a KWL chart (see page 47) as a way to reteach and assess what kids know.
- *Hook into prior learning.* Connect the concept being retaught to a similar story or concepts kids have already mastered. Better yet, connect and apply the concept to something the kids value highly.
- *Practice.* Sometimes kids just need practice. So give them opportunities to practice in a variety of fun ways. Try flash cards, matching games, speaking into a toy microphone (kids think a capped, whiteboard marker is a mighty fine pretend microphone), puppets, Bible action figures, or other techniques.

When reteaching, remember the promise Jesus gives in John 14:26:

> But the Helper, the Holy Spirit, whom the Father will send in My name, He will teach you all things, and bring to your remembrance all that I said to you. (NASB)

When it seems that efforts to reteach have failed, ask God to honor His promise through the work of the Holy Spirit in the hearts of kids with special needs. He can be counted upon to keep it.

Strategy 8—Planning for Success at the Craft Table

A wise college special education professor once said, "Remember that the kids in your class struggle in almost every aspect of their lives. Turning in a pretty paper might seem trivial, but for these kids, it can make a huge difference in their sense of competence."

With the proliferation of technology in schools, we put pen to paper a lot less these days. However, children still need to flex those developing muscles to achieve a number of small-motor tasks such as cutting and shoe tying. And, regardless of the available technology for writing activities at school, kids still participate in crafts that are meaningful to them. When creating a gift for a parent or a card for a missionary, it's hard for many kids with disabilities to make their paper as pretty as they'd like. Fortunately, we can plan ahead to increase the likelihood of success with a few modifications:

Offer Step-by-Step Directions—Step by Step

This sounds so obvious, doesn't it? Of course we explain each step of our crafts to kids. It's important to remember, though, that some kids have difficulty sequencing directions or recalling the steps. For multi-step projects, it's best to give directions one or two at a time.

Get Spaced-Out Children with disabilities may need more room to work. This might help them focus, or provide the elbow room they need to work comfortably. If possible, provide additional workspace and allow kids to choose a spot that feels right.

Provide Visual Support Kids on the autism spectrum rely heavily on visual cues. If possible, have a sample of each step of your craft on the table, or do the craft along with them so they can see what you are doing.

Have Extras Handy Children with weaker fine motor skills, sensory difficulties, or poor visual-motor abilities may press too hard, ripping the paper, or run out of room on the page. Therefore, they may need a do-over. Reminding kids at the beginning of the activity that you have extra materials just in case can be a huge relief and may reduce the possibility of a frustrated meltdown.

Consider Products to Make Things Easier Some kids with hidden disabilities have a hard time sitting still for a variety of reasons. Several products are available to make doing so easier. One helpful product is a slant board. This can help kids focus and also reduce fatigue when writing or coloring. They can sometimes be a bit pricey; a large three-ring binder can provide similar support.

For more information on the products mentioned, please visit the following sites. Type the product in the website's search box.

www.therapro.com

www.therapyshoppe.com

www.enasco.com

www.amazon.com

Another product for seat work is a specialized cushion. These wedges or discs give children a bit more sensory input so they can fidget without floundering. They're also a bit expensive, but can be quite helpful.

Also, stocking your craft cabinet with different sized crayons and pencils, both the fat and skinny kinds, as well as offering inexpensive pencil grippers allow for more comfortable writing and drawing.

Finally, remember that some kids prefer to stand while doing crafts—and that's okay.

Strategy 9—Raised-Line Paper and Other Writing Tools

For some students who have disabilities, writing can be a tedious and frustrating task. This can be attributed to any number of issues: visual-motor integration, problems with attention, sequential or spacing issues, and language disabilities are just a few.

Whatever the underlying issue may be, lack of neatness is a common symptom. Although handwriting is not often a top priority in today's keyboard-driven world, kids are still asked to complete handwritten assignments on a fairly regular basis. This is also true at church. When students struggle with this, they become acutely aware that their papers don't look as nice as those of their peers. Poorly formed letters and eraser smudges make their papers look sloppy. Although we might argue that some of the world's brightest minds produce the messiest handwriting, the fact remains that turning in a pretty paper is important to children.

How Raised-Line Paper Can Help

One way to assist students in this endeavor is by offering raised-line paper. The lines on this paper are embossed, which raises them slightly. This provides both visual and tactile cues for students who have difficulty with letter formation, spacing and staying in the lines. As students write, they will feel the lines both with their fingers and through the motion of their pencils. This may help students to form letters and words more accurately, increasing their feeling of success with writing tasks.

How to Introduce Raised-Line Paper

When using this kind of tool in your classroom, it's best to provide it for everyone if possible. This will help class projects or bulletin boards look uniform in appearance. More importantly, kids with disabilities will have an opportunity to see that they are using the same materials as their peers. Already acutely aware that they struggle with writing, they don't need to be self-conscious about using different paper than everyone else. In order to save money, kids can use scrap paper or regular paper for writing or dictating rough drafts, and then use the raised-line paper for final copies if necessary.

> Raised-line paper can be found in the following places:
> * The Therapy Shoppe (www.therapyshoppe.com)
> * Beyond Play (www.beyondplay.com)
> * Pacific Pediatric Supply (www.pacificpediatricsupply.com)
>
> Type "raised-line paper" in the search engine on each website to get pricing and shipping information.

Strategy 10—Managing Behavior: Proximity Control

Put yourself in this scenario: You are standing at the front of your class, introducing a new concept. You have told the students the schedule for the day, and you have reiterated your expectations. As you delve into the lesson, however, you notice little Stephen in the middle of the room. His shock of red hair, twinkly eyes, and quick smile make him a welcome addition to your class—if only he could pay attention for more than thirty consecutive seconds.

As you continue teaching, it is impossible to ignore Stephen's current project. He's tearing his worksheet into a pile of confetti which he covertly sprinkles into the hair of the girl in front of him. He isn't being malicious. Knowing Stephen, you probably can guess that he thinks the snow will look really pretty in her curls, and it reminds him of a sledding trip he took with his grandpa. He's off-task, and Emma, the girl with the curls, has noticed and is getting annoyed. What should you do?

Why to Use Proximity Control

In this situation, it might be easy to blurt out, "Stephen, stop it!" After all, you have probably reminded him fourteen times to get back on task. Instead, try a strategy called "proximity control." This simply means that as you continue teaching, you slowly, but deliberately walk around your room stopping purposefully near Stephen. Children like Stephen, who struggle with impulse control, are very likely to sense your presence, stop what they're doing, and refocus their attention.

Benefits of Proximity Control

By using this strategy, you accomplish several things:

- *You preserve Stephen's dignity.* You have not embarrassed him in front of his peers.
- *You maintain the attention of the rest of the students* and continue teaching your content.
- *You subtly reinforce your leadership* in the classroom without frightening your wiggly friend.
- *You reinforce respect and fairness* for the students and the materials in the classroom.

Most importantly, you help Stephen—and all of your students—remember that church is a place where everyone is welcome and everyone is safe.

Strategy 11—Tips for Transitions

Anyone who has taught kids knows how hard it can be to help them transition to a time of learning. Whether they're bouncing after a rowdy worship session, or just plain excited because it's snowing outside, kids sometimes need help settling down.

About ten years ago, Katie had a class of all boys. The energy level was high almost all of the time, and transitions were particularly difficult. This was a self-contained class for kids with special needs, and at least half of the students struggled with maintaining attention. Katie felt she spent most of the day directing them (okay, nagging and pleading) to settle down and get some work done. She periodically tape-recorded class to analyze her interactions with the kids. She was appalled at how much nagging she did. No wonder the boys were tuning her out.

A Football Fan Is Born

During that same year, she became interested in football. The Washington Redskins were doing well, and she got caught up in the excitement. She and her husband, along with their friends, spent Sunday afternoons in front of the television during game time. She didn't know a lot about football and spent a good deal of time whispering, "What's that signal for?" or "Why did the ref do that?"

A Teaching Strategy Is Born

Katie wondered if, somehow, football might be able to help with transition problems. As football season continued, she became quite savvy with the football signals, and took great pride in learning the meaning of even the most obscure motions. One day after the boys returned from recess in super-high-energy-mode, she gave them a try. Instead of nagging or yelling, she stood silently at the front of the room and began going through some of the football signals. One by one, they noticed what she was doing and began piping up, "Safety! Holding! Touchdown!"

A Transition Tool Is Born

This activity became a great transition tool. The students learned that when Katie started doing football signals, she needed their attention: eyes up front, bodies seated and ready to learn. It might work for the children you're working with, too, even if their favorite football team isn't the Redskins.

Football signals aren't the only way to help kids refocus and transition. Try these:

- *Marble jars.* When students transition quietly and efficiently, put a marble in a large jar. When the jar is full, the class can have a special celebration for working together.
- *Sing a song.* Music is a great way to signal transition time. Pair transition activities with songs so kids know, when they hear you start to sing, that it is time to move to the next activity.
- *Paper chains.* When you notice kids working together and showing good manners during transitions or other times, offer them a thin strip of paper. At the end of class, add those strips of paper to an existing paper chain to represent the care and kindness kids have shown to each other.
- *Follow the leader.* Allow students an opportunity to lead transition time. This allows the class to work as a community and lead each other, which has great benefits for the kingdom.

Chapter 7

Party Time Treats: Ideas for Holidays and Holy Days

oliday parties and holy day celebrations are automatic excitement-generators for kids. To corral the energy of kids eagerly anticipating—and sometimes secretly stressing about—special events and accompanying changes in routine, ministry workers need to be prepared ahead of time. They need to deal with possible pitfalls long before the party begins. This chapter alerts children's ministry workers to common pitfalls for kids with special needs: church pageants, gift-making projects, inviting one and all to special events, making parties accessible and fun, preparing kids for the party, food allergies, and party manners.

Parties and celebrations are part of childhood. Every child, whatever his or her special need may be, should be included in the celebrations that mark the Christian faith. Celebrations that shine a light on the joy believers have in Christ. Celebrations of hope that make hearts beat faster and give a glimpse of the enchantment waiting for all of us in heaven.

A Prayer of Celebration

*Lord, thank You for holy days and holidays, for times
to celebrate Your goodness in this world and the hope of*

heaven yet to come. Open my eyes to any obstacles that could keep a child from being part of these celebrations. Open my eyes to the solution and give me the energy and wisdom to eliminate those obstacles. Use this time of celebration to draw children closer to You.

Strategy 1—Preparing for the Church Pageant

In churches during Advent, we see little kids dressed up as angels, parading in and creating a Christmas tableau. Chubby fingers clutch shepherd's crooks, and toothless grins grace the faces of Wise Men as they seek out their parents in the congregation.

Church Pageant Jitters

And, in churches everywhere on Friday night, parents of children with hidden disabilities pray fervently.

Dear God, Please don't let my kid have a meltdown.

Please calm his nerves, God, so he can play his part without crying.

God, please help her control herself so she doesn't smack the little blonde kid.

Please, God. Please let us just get through this performance. Please.

So much tension surrounds church pageants. Changes in routine, lack of sleep and social demands can create a Bermuda-triangle effect despite the most careful planning. It seems that this is often a time for re-grieving as parents cope with their children's special needs, all the while attempting normalcy at school, in the neighborhood, with relatives, and at church.

How to Calm Those Church Pageant Jitters

These preparations can make the church pageant go more smoothly:

- *Invite parents* to bring their child to the church sometime during the week to review the pageant. This breeds familiarity and comfort.

- *Reserve seats* for parents of kids who may struggle with the performance. This way, if a child is showing signs of needing a break or a quick escape, parents have easy access to him/her and can assist without compromising the child's dignity.
- *Write a social story* (see page 102) that outlines the experience of participating in the Christmas Pageant.
- *Be kind to yourself* and heed the words of our friend, Barb Dittrich of Snappin' Ministries, "Good enough is good enough." The pageant won't be perfect. Not just because of your child's behavior, but for a variety of reasons. And remember, with a bunch of sheep and some bewildered shepherds, that first Christmas probably didn't feel very perfect, either.
- *Recruit extra volunteers as you finalize preparations.* Sometimes just having a few extra bodies near the kids as they find their places can provide the structure and safety needed. This is not a time to introduce a new buddy to a child with special needs, nor is it necessary to host a training session. The objective here is to help keep the peace and order. Many times, high school or middle school kids are willing to pitch in for this small time commitment.
- *Be specific and succinct* with your directions, using encouraging language. For example, "I notice that our fifth graders really know how to keep hands to themselves." Or, "I see that the choir remembers our two rules: hands to self, quiet voices backstage."
- *Offer to help with driving to the church.* Sometimes kids who have hidden disabilities need a bit of quiet time, or one-to-one time, with a parent before a performance; sharing a car ride with an excited set of siblings or friends can upset the applecart. An opportunity to divide and conquer with carpooling can set everyone up for success.
- *Offer to watch a child at home or church.* If a child elects not to participate or is unable to join in because of illness or any other reason, offer to watch the child in church, or even at home, while the parents enjoy worshipping with their other children.
- *Show appreciation for all of the children's efforts.* Kids, and their parents, love when grandmas and grandpas gush over a job well done. Be generous and specific with your praise, knowing how much effort has gone into participating in worship.

It may not be a silent night at your church pageant. But with God's family together, it will be a holy night.

Strategy 2—Easy-to-Make Gifts

Children love to make and give gifts. This desire is evidence that we are created in the image of God, the Giver of all gifts. We can foster this desire by encouraging kids to make gifts to commemorate holidays like Christmas, Valentine's Day, Mother's Day, Father's Day, and Grandparent's Day.

Gifts That Rise to the Challenge

The challenge when selecting gifts for children to make is to choose projects that can be made independently by children with special needs and are still appropriate for their typically developing peers. Activities that meet that criteria have several things in common. You'll know you've found one if it meets several of the commonalities listed below:

- *A few simple steps.* Easy-to-make gifts have three or four steps to complete a basic model.
- *Room for embellishment.* Once the basic gift is finished, can kids who finish quickly add more decoration?
- *Easy-to-manipulate materials.* Choose projects that use materials easy for kids to handle, especially for children with special needs who may have difficulty with fine motor or eye-hand coordination. Select big beads instead of small ones, craft foam instead of thin paper, large crayons or markers along with smaller ones. Also, have adaptive scissors on hand for kids who need them and glue sticks instead of squeeze glue bottles.
- *Steps that can be completed ahead of time.* If a project has too many steps, some—like cutting or painting—can be completed by volunteers. When the children arrive, they can do the rest on their own.
- *Premade materials.* Look for projects that use some premade materials: painted boxes or picture frames instead of unfinished ones, punch-out pieces rather than cutouts, premade beads instead of making them from scratch with clay.

Gifts That Build Skills

Certain kinds of handmade gifts actually help kids with special needs build their skills. Stringing beads to make a necklace or bracelet develops a child's grasping muscles and improves eye-hand coordination. So does peeling stickers and putting them on a different surface. These activities are easy to adapt for different skill levels. Provide a selection of beads of different sizes so kids can choose ones they can handle easily. Have craft foam stickers along with paper ones so children can again self-select materials at their own skill levels.

Gifts Loved Ones Adore

Two final pieces of advice can simplify the search for easy-to-make gifts. First, remember that parents adore gifts that preserve a glimpse of their children at their present age. So photographs of kids in simple foam or popsicle frames or glued into a bottle cap and made into a refrigerator magnet are always appreciated. As are gifts that incorporate hand tracings and painted handprints, footprints, thumb and finger prints, and the timeless plaster of paris imprint of a child's hand or foot. Second, keep your eyes open throughout the year for easy-to-make gift ideas. Keep them in a file, or bookmark the URL on your computer, to avoid panic as holidays approach. With that in mind, the sidebar has a few ideas to get you started.

Websites with Easy-to-Make Gift Ideas for Kids

Christmas:
http://www.parentmap.com/article/15-homemade-christmas-gifts-that-kids-can-make

http://www.ivillage.ca/parenting/easy-crafts-kids/homemade-christmas-gifts

Mother's Day:
http://www.buzzfeed.com/donnad/easy-emergency-mothers-day-crafts-for-kids

Father's Day:
http://www.parenting.com/gallery/7-easy-to-make-gifts-for-fathers-day

Strategy 3—Party Fun and Food Allergies

Kids with food allergies are told "no" often. "No, you can't eat at McDonald's. No, you can't have corn on the cob. No ice cream cone for you. No honey, those pretzels aren't gluten-free. No, don't eat that until I check the label."

Sure, kids adjust. And sure, by the age of five or six they understand the importance of avoiding foods that cause physical discomfort, affect emotions and behavior, or are life-threatening. But kids are still kids and come party time, they want to enjoy the same fun treats as their peers.

The good news is that because the prevalence of food allergies has increased in recent decades, it's easier to find products allergy sufferers can eat. The bad news is that finding enough foods safe for all kids can be tricky. Here are a few suggestions about how to put on a party spread everyone can enjoy and eat.

Talk to parents. Ask parents about the severity of a child's food allergy and for tips about how to avoid food that provokes allergic reactions. Talk to them about suggestions for party foods. Request recipes they've created and invite them to provide treats they know are safe. Also find out symptoms the child will exhibit if a food allergen is inadvertently consumed and what to do if that happens.

Hit the glitz. For kids, half the fun of a party is the sparkle. So use glitzy plates, napkins, and cups. Decorate the table with flair. All the eye candy may make up for the lack of sugar-laden treats.

Serve whole foods rather than processed ones. Whole foods are those made with just one ingredient. Think fruits, veggies, chicken breasts, hamburger. Whole foods aren't hiding potential allergens, so they are safe to eat. And if a child is allergic to a whole food such as grapes or cantaloupe, it can be easily avoided.

Read labels. Check the ingredient list on the labels on processed foods such as crackers, snack items, cake mixes, and canned frosting. Avoid products containing food allergens. Since 2004, companies have been required by the FDA to very clearly restate the presence of eight major food allergens (milk, egg, fish, crustacean shellfish, tree nuts, wheat, peanuts, and soybeans) at the end of the label's ingredient list. But careful reading is required for all other allergens. (See the sidebar for more information.) Also watch for the words "Made in a facility that processes milk, eggs, nuts, or other known allergens." Children with life-threatening food allergies can't have those items either.

Quiz restaurants and bakeries. If treats are ordered from a restaurant or bakery, inquire about the ingredients used. Many chain restaurants provide ingredient lists for their menus upon request. But if they don't, ask the food server or manager to find the information needed. If they can't help, look elsewhere.

Offer an alternative. If it's impossible to create an allergen-free party spread, provide a suitable alternative to the child who has to abstain from some foods. Substitute a dairy-free frozen treat for ice cream, a gluten-free cupcake as garishly decorated as the wheat-based ones, almonds instead of peanuts (or vice versa), and so on.

Shine the spotlight on games and activities. Make games and activities the main event of the party instead of the food. Concentrate on games that everyone can participate in, enjoy, and remember long after the food memories fade away.

Food Allergies Common in Children

- *Eggs* and products that contain eggs or dried eggs.
- *Dairy* encompasses milk, butter, ice cream, yogurt, buttermilk, sour cream, whey, cheese, and products containing any of those ingredients.
- *Casein,* a protein found in dairy.
- *Gluten,* found in wheat and some other grains.
- *Peanuts* or products containing peanuts or made with peanut oil.
- *Tree nuts* or products containing nuts or tree nut oil.
- *Corn* and products containing corn, corn meal, corn oil, corn starch, corn syrup, or high fructose corn syrup.
- *Soy* and products made with soy such as soy sauce, tofu, soy beans, or soy oil.

Strategy 4—Party Manners

Elbows off the table.
Ladies first.
Chew with your mouth closed.
Don't interrupt.
Use your manners!

Good manners can be a tricky and abstract concept for kids. After all, what is permitted at the home might not be appropriate for a restaurant or Aunt Opal's house. Good manners on the playground would not necessarily be the same as the expectations for good manners in the theater. Expectations for good manners can change depending on the situation and on the age or experience of the individual. At a dinner party, kids might be expected to wait until everyone is served before eating; at a football game, they can begin eating as soon as they have purchased their hot dog. Babies may spit out food they dislike, while older children might be scolded for this. When we want students in our programs to display good manners, we must teach them explicitly and communicate clearly. The following examples provide ideas about how to do that.

List Expectations

If we plan to take our class into the sanctuary to watch a baptism, we need to list our expectations. When we go into the sanctuary, we:

- Stay with our class
- Keep our mouths quiet
- Listen to the pastor

Practice Manners

If possible, we can take students into the sanctuary when no one is there and allow them to rehearse their behavior. This can alleviate anxiety for kids, and also reinforce the kind of behavior you would like to see.

Review Expectations

As we prepare kids for a variety of events, we need to remember that thorough instructions and a review of expectations can set everyone up for success. If the class is sharing a meal together, review the kind of manners expected. Reminding kids to be polite can be abstract and frustrating for them while "napkins in laps, and quiet chewing" gives kids specific ways to show good manners.

Emphasize Caring

Explain that we use good manners as a way to care for others. Kids who have difficulty with perspective-taking might have trouble with this concept. However, reminders about how our good manners make others feel happy and comfortable can help them to develop habits that will make a difference in their relationships both in and out of the church.

Strategy 5—Party Fun for Everyone

"My daughter is six years old, and has never been invited to a birthday party." A young mother's voice quavered as she continued. "Yes, she's medically fragile and blind. But she's also a little girl. And she loves birthday parties."

Many, many parents of kids with diverse special needs tell a similar story. Their kids have never gone to another child's birthday party, a Christmas party at someone else's house, or a block party in their neighborhood. Why? Because they've never been invited.

The lack of invitations are rarely due to spite or deliberate exclusion. They are more often due to thoughtlessness, ignorance about how to include everyone, or the inability to look past a disability to see the child living with it.

The church has an opportunity to rectify the situation by inviting all children to participate in celebrations put on within children's ministry. Thoughtful planning before the invitations are issued can make the party accessible to every child. Because parents may be delighted and a little worried about how their kids will handle their first party, forethought will also prepare the hosts to respond to FAQs about a variety of party concerns.

Party FAQs

Transportation. By planning ahead of time, car pools can be organized or the church van reserved to pick up children whose parents can't bring them.

Access. For a party at someone's home, check for easy access by wheelchair or a walker. Also be sure the child can get to the bathroom and manipulate the fixtures.

Activities. Plan a mix of games: rambunctious, quiet, skill-based, chance-based, gross motor, fine motor, individual, pairs, small teams, and larger teams, so every child can participate in something.

Party plans. If you have children who thrive on routine, take time to send a party plan to the parents. This will help everyone know what to expect.

Treats. Choose foods friendly to kids with allergies. (See *Party Fun and Food Allergies* on page 119.)

Supervision. Arrange for extra adults to attend the party. Consider extending an invitation for the parent of a child with special needs to be at the party. This could be the deciding factor for medically fragile children who are on ventilators or use feeding tubes.

Quiet room. Prepare a quiet room, or nook, ahead of time. Let all the kids know it's there in case they need a break from the action. (See *Creating Quiet Zones*, page 21.)

Other Party Accommodations

These strategies can make the party a pleasurable experience for everyone:

Give children something to do. The beginning of a party can be a little awkward as people arrive one by one, or in small groups. Puzzles, a homemade photo booth, or art supplies can all provide a way for guests to avoid anxiety-producing small talk.

Offer kids a leadership role in the party. For some children, having some control may be comforting. Ask them to serve as greeters, servers, or game hosts. Allow them time to practice these roles in advance.

Provide choices. While many kids love Dance Dance Revolution, along with loud music, others may prefer listening to a story or drawing a picture. Offering options lets kids find their comfort zone.

Be wary of outer space. When giving a party, we often want to move our class to a larger space, with more room to play and run. This can work well, as long as clear boundaries are given, and a supervised, small-room option is available for kids who need a cozier environment.

Plan a shorter time than you think you need. While parties can be fun, we don't want too much of a good thing. Try to set a timeframe that will allow everyone to leave the party while they're still having fun.

Simple Strategies for a Successful Party

- Have a visual timer handy so a reluctant party-goer knows how long each activity, or the entire party, will last. (See *Visual Timers*, page 101.)
- Create a visual schedule ahead of time. Review it beforehand and have it at the party for the child to review as needed. (See *Visual Schedules*, page 40.)
- Create a social story for the child to read and review before attending the big event. (See *Social Stories*, page 102.)
- If the child has a peer buddy, arrange for that person to attend also. (See *Peer Training*, page 61.)
- Have headphones handy for a child who's easily overwhelmed by loud noises.

Depending on the special needs of the children invited to the party, other accommodations can be made. The accommodations already being used in other children's ministry settings may be easy to transfer to a party setting. If not, ask the parent for suggestions.

And always, always have a camera handy. Because when the party guests arrive, you will want to capture their joy at being included in one of childhood's great delights. Party time!

Strategy 6—How to Handle the Crucifixion Story

The details of Christ's crucifixion are enough to disturb the sleep of mature believers who understand the concepts of propitiation, substitutionary sacrifice, and redemption. Imagine the effect of a recounting of the cruelties He bore on a thirteen-year-old child with developmental delays and the emotional sensitivity of a five-year-old. Think of how a child with autism and a fascination with all things bloody could obsess about the beatings Jesus endured. Consider how dwelling on the helplessness of Christ on the cross could shatter any sense of security in a child with anxiety.

And yet, the death of Jesus and His resurrection make the Christian faith different from any other. So how much of that story should be shared with children with special needs? And how should those details be conveyed? How do children's ministry volunteers know when enough is enough? Here are some guidelines to assist in answering those questions:

Use Kid Language

Many young children and those with developmental delays don't understand the permanency of death, or haven't experienced the death of someone they love. But they have experienced pain, hunger, tiredness, being cold, and being alone and will understand the Good Friday story in those terms.

Focus on the Results

Focus on the results of Jesus' death rather than the details of it. The bloody, gory details of the crucifixion don't need to be shared with anxious children, children who are young or have developmental delays, and kids already overly fascinated with blood and gore. Dwelling on those details could cause kids to fixate on them to the exclusion of Christ's resurrection. A better tactic would be to say that Jesus loved us and died for our sins so we could live with Him forever.

Talk About All of Holy Week

Give other events of Holy Week their due. Mention Palm Sunday, the Last Supper, Jesus praying in the garden, Good Friday, and the resurrection. These events show children that Jesus knew what was happening and was looking forward to the resurrection.

Acknowledge Emotions

If kids feel sad that Jesus had to die for our sins, let them know it's okay to feel that way. Jesus' friends were very sad after he died. But their sadness turned to joy when He rose from the dead.

These guidelines, applied to the special needs of the kids served by children's ministry, help churches fulfill the command of Jesus in Matthew 19:14 to let the children come to Him. When Jesus gave that command, and in every recorded interaction He had with children, He was whole and unbloodied. Perhaps because He knew little children need a Savior who holds them safe until they are ready to comprehend the events of the crucifixion, and the victory of the cross.

Chapter 8

Service with a Smile: Teaching Children to Serve at Church

L et's say you receive an invitation to supper at the home of an acquaintance you've just met. You also receive an invitation from long-time friends to eat with them on a different evening. You're excited and, you admit, a little nervous about the first invitation. But the second? Going to your friends' home for supper feels almost like going home. And you know why. It's because you've spent time in their home, rocking their babies so the new mama could take a nap. Running the wet-vac in their basement after a flood several years back. Painting their house as part of a service group from church. Not only that, but those friends volunteered to assemble the tent in your backyard and man it during your daughter's graduation party. They stayed at your house with your kids the night your dad died. And they pitched in when your roof needed new shingles. A meal at their house feels almost like going home because you're more than guests. You're fellow servants.

Kids with special needs should be invited to church. However, they shouldn't remain guests forever. At some point, once they feel acclimated and included, they need to do more than be served by the church. They need to serve it, too.

Now, kids aren't likely to begin serving on their own. They may not know what to do. They may not even know they are allowed to serve. But children's ministry workers are in a position to open the service door and walk them through it. This chapter helps volunteers do just that. It contains ideas and logistical information about how kids—and adults—with special needs can serve the church on Sundays, on special service days, and throughout the week.

Kids with special needs, who are often the recipients of many special services, should be given the opportunity to serve, also. They have gifts to share with the body of Christ. By encouraging kids to serve, they are more likely to view the church as their second home.

A Prayer of Service

Lord, give me a humble heart that is willing to serve and be served by others. Give me the ability to encourage these children to serve, so they believe they can give to others. Give me words to share Christ with them so they love Him enough to follow His example of service. Give our group opportunities to serve so each one here feels at home in this church.

Strategy 1—Involving Kids in Church Ministries

"Young people are not the future of the church," pastor and youth ministry expert Michelle Thomas-Bush says emphatically. "Young people are the church."

We often forget this simple truth, as though children are like delicate pastries that we allow to rise before kneading carefully, shaping, and molding. Our care for them is well-placed, and necessary, as well. Kids need our guidance and our wisdom. However, when we focus solely on what we can do for them, we communicate that service is for grown-ups only.

Identify Gifts

Every child—every person—has unique and special talents to offer the kingdom. One of our greatest tasks as teachers and leaders is to help kids identify their gifts and provide them an opportunity to use those gifts to serve others. For kids with disabilities, the invitation to serve may come as a surprise. During the week, these children spend time working on their deficits, and are often left out of special opportunities for leadership and service. Church can—and should—be different. It should be a place where differences are celebrated as a means to serving the body.

Encourage Service

As we consider how to encourage kids to serve, it is important to remember that some children may gain more from serving than from sitting in small groups. For example, one little boy, diagnosed with ADHD, struggled to maintain attention for the entire seventy-five-minute Sunday school class. To remedy this, his parents and a pastor worked together to create a solution that would benefit him and the church. After forty-five minutes of class, he would don an orange parking vest and head out to the parking lot with the rest of the traffic team. There, he would stand next to an adult and direct the second service traffic toward parking spaces. He did it with a great smile and much enthusiasm, blessing both the traffic team and the families arriving at church.

Consider Opportunities

Many opportunities for service exist for kids in our congregations. Some children prefer social opportunities, like ushering or helping with a younger class of children, while others prefer behind-the-scenes or independent work in the church office or backstage. Consider the following:

- Greeting guests
- Escorting new families to their classrooms
- Assisting with coffee/tea service
- Helping the tech team with PowerPoint and sound
- Participating in the choir
- Making bulletin boards
- Helping with administrative tasks like folding bulletins and organizing mail
- Creating cards or writing letters to members who are sick

We want children, including those with disabilities, to participate fully in the life of the church when they become adults. The best way to make this happen is by creating opportunities to serve while they are young, so that they can internalize their worth to the kingdom. Our parking attendant certainly learned this. His mother, when asked about her son's involvement, said simply, "That is his ministry."

Strategy 2—Tech Day: Kids Helping Others with Technology

When we plan service or outreach events in our churches, we should consider the needs of those being served, and the strengths of those serving. Often, we can find unique ways for our kids to serve others by tapping into the kids' unique gifts.

Out-of-the-Box Service

A church in Ohio found an out-of-the-box way for students to serve their church family: a tech support day. Adults in the congregation were invited to take their laptops, tablets, and smart phones to church, where they received free tech tutoring from the students in the middle and high school youth groups. The adults welcomed the help in mastering their digital world. And, for the kids, it was not only an opportunity to serve, but also to shine.

As we reflect on this project, it's easy to see why this might be a great way for kids with disabilities to serve. Many kids have an exceptional gift for understanding and enjoying technology, and are often eager to talk about it. This event would give kids with that profile a chance to showcase their gifts. This not only helps the adults receiving the service, but also demonstrates this special skill to typically developing peers. Some of the peers will be impressed, and begin to realize that they have more in common than they originally thought, potentially helping kids to start or deepen friendships.

How to Plan a Tech Day

To plan a tech support day at your church, use the following checklist:

- *Reserve a large room* or a group of smaller rooms.
- *Have extension cords* and plenty of power strips available.
- *Recruit volunteers* who can circulate to offer support if kids become anxious or tired; be aware that some students might become frustrated if they think the person they are helping isn't getting it quickly enough.
- *Recruit more volunteers* who can provide one-to-one support to kids who need it.
- *Offer breaks* to students who may need it, or suggest a shorter shift if that would be most successful.

Remember that not every student will enjoy working with adults; some may prefer to simply demonstrate. That is okay. Offer space for them to do this. Finally, all students may not wish to join the tech part of this outreach. Some may prefer to make refreshments or act as receptionists. No matter what the service activity, everyone has something to offer.

Strategy 3—Serving Throughout the Week

Because so many church service opportunities are available on Sunday morning, it's easy to develop tunnel vision and overlook ways to serve the rest of the week. But many churches have midweek activities, and all churches require regular maintenance and preparation for Sunday mornings. Those kinds of volunteer opportunities may be a better fit for children and teens with sensory issues. They may function better in the quieter and less crowded weekday atmosphere. Serving during the week widens their perspective of what church life entails, and it connects them to people and tasks that aren't visible on Sunday morning.

That lack of visibility can make it hard to root out service opportunities and match them to kids eager to participate. But with a little detective work and persistence, the invisible becomes visible, and viable ways emerge for kids with special needs to serve.

Raise Awareness

Communication is the key to raising your awareness of where kids can serve and to inform others of an eager workforce. First, talk to parents to explain the idea, get permission, and to check schedules and transportation. Then call the pastor, ministry leaders, the church secretary or administrative assistant, and the custodial staff to ask them what jobs need to be done and to tell them about kids who would like to serve.

Safety First

Safety is always a first priority for kids and adults. So be sure any adults supervising child volunteers have passed a background check. If the work isn't done in a highly visible area, arrange for two adults (not married to each other) to supervise.

Make a Match

Place children in service areas that maximize their strengths. A one-time opportunity to paint the outside of the church may be best for an energetic child who's easily distracted. A child who thrives with routine could be perfect for the weekly task of folding bulletins. A teen who can work independently could vacuum the worship area, while an adolescent who needs supervision could stuff envelopes in the office.

Train Everyone

Both the adults supervising and the child may need initial training. Adults may appreciate tips about how much direction is needed, how to best communicate, what triggers a child's meltdowns, and how to handle them. The child also needs on-the-job training to learn expectations and how to complete the work.

Follow Up

Once a child or teen has had time to settle into volunteer service, check with the child, the parents, and the supervisor to see how things are going. Listen carefully and make adjustments so kids with special needs can serve with excellence.

When kids serve beyond Sunday mornings on a regular basis, the body of Christ is no longer doing church for them. The body is doing church with them and is fulfilling Paul's admonition to honor the unique contribution of every member created by God to do His work.

Weekday Service Possibilities at Church

- Folding bulletins
- Delivering Sunday school papers and supplies to classrooms
- Stuffing and stamping envelopes
- Yard work
- Snow removal
- Painting
- Simple repairs
- Routine cleaning
- Greeter at midweek activities
- Selecting books for younger kids at story time
- Praying for people on the prayer request list
- Writing notes to people in the hospital

Strategy 4—Match 'Em Up: Pairing Mentors with Kids

Learning to serve in the church is a lot like learning to cook. Kids with special needs learn service best by working one-on-one with a mentor willing to invest time and patience in their lives. So matching children with mentors willing to teach them how to serve is a good way to launch them into service. One key to creating successful service relationships is careful matching of kids with mentors.

Where to Start

Safety is always the place to start in children's ministry. Therefore, potential mentors must undergo and pass a background check before being matched with kids. Second, potential mentors should have a desire to mentor a child with special needs. If they are reluctant or feel unequipped, offer on-the-job training in another special needs ministry setting such as serving as an assistant in an inclusive Sunday school class. Or partner them with an already equipped adult with special needs in some other service area. Then wait until the potential mentor feels ready for a one-on-one situation to make a match.

How to Make a Match

To successfully match kids with special needs to potential mentors, get to know both parties and look for what could make a good relationship.

- *Age and gender.* Some children respond better to certain age groups or genders than others, so match them accordingly. Also, if a child tends to make unhealthy attachments to people of a certain age or gender, avoid those matches.
- *Professional experience.* Does the mentor have professional skills that make a difference? A mentor with medical training could be a wise choice for a child with a medical condition that requires a practiced eye. A teacher with specialized training might be the right person to work with a child with significant behavior challenges.
- *Personal experience.* Someone who has a neighbor, relative, or friend with a special need could be a good match for a child with a similar condition.
- *Personality.* High energy, impulsive children need energetic mentors who are also calm. Shy, introverted children can be overwhelmed by a talkative go-getter, but blossom if paired with mentors who quietly work side-by-side with them.
- *Hobbies and shared interests.* Some children with special needs are fascinated, almost obsessed, by certain topics. Connecting them with someone who's an expert in the area could be a positive for both of them.
- *Schedule.* Nothing tanks a good mentor match quicker than conflicting schedules. Make sure that the child and the mentor can meet on a regular basis with few interruptions.

- *Prayer.* God has a track record of doing what humans think is impossible. So lift up potential matches in prayer and listen carefully for God's approval, or for an unexpected divine pairing.

How to Provide Support

Once kids have been matched to mentors, the odds of creating successful relationship can be increased by providing support. Call now and then to see how things are going. Come alongside to offer training. Brainstorm and trouble-shoot problems together. Serve the mentors so they can serve kids so they can serve the church. And eventually, after a consistent investment of time and patience, the body of Christ will learn to cook.

Chapter 9

Washing Up:
Strategies for Successfully
Wrapping Up an Activity

ehind every successful dinner party there's a successful exit
strategy engineered by a host who knows how to wind down
the evening and send guests on their way. The guests may
be clueless, unaware of the cues that gracefully ended the evening
without a word being said. They may not be quite sure why the taxi
arrived at exactly the right moment, or why they're going home with
carefully wrapped leftovers to eat for lunch tomorrow. But the host
knows. Indeed the host intentionally orchestrated the details of the
departure so the guests left the party safe, happy, and eager to return.

Without carefully engineered departure strategies in place, we
will be tempted to open the door and send kids on their way when
the hour is up. To avoid that temptation, special attention must be
paid to preparing kids with special needs for the many transitions
faced at departure time. This chapter is a smorgasbord of ideas to help
kids navigate those transitions. Ideas to create a departure routine by
judicial use of videos, books, wall timers, centers, and music. Ways
to lower anxiety and calm kids who had a bad morning, or while

they wait for their parents. Strategies to increase anticipation for next time. Procedures to ensure safety as kids leave. And tips about how to communicate with parents at pick-up time or via the Internet about behavior concerns, upcoming events, and the day's lesson.

Last impressions create a *lasting* impression for both kids with special needs and their parents. By engineering a safe and happy departure time for kids and parents, they are likely to leave with the last impression of being valued and loved. With the lasting impression imprinted on their hearts, they want to come back to this place again and again.

A Prayer of Parting

Father, I will be tired by the end of my time with these children. Give me energy, strength, and wisdom to last until the children are safely on their way. When I want to let down my guard, give me a heart to put the children first. Help me calm their anxieties, celebrate their accomplishments, and keep them safe. May they sense how much You value and love them through my actions and words.

Strategy 1—Safe and Smooth Checkout Times

Come checkout time, you're worn out. The kids are tired. And everybody's hungry and eager to go home and relax. The temptation to lower your guard and send the kids on their way can be overwhelming. To resist the temptation, try implementing this five-step process to maintain your program's standards until the last child is safely on the way home.

Step One: Be Prepared
A week or two before your program or Sunday school year begins, look over the registration forms completed by the parents. If you have questions or concerns, talk to the parents for clarification. Send parents a letter or email describing checkout protocol and encourage them to contact you with questions.

Use information on the registration forms to create a checkout notebook, one page per child. On each child's page, record a contact phone number, address, and who has permission to pick up the child. Keep the notebook in your classroom, or wherever you wait with the kids during checkout time. Also note any restrictions on who should not pick up a child. Some churches house this information in a computerized check-in/checkout program and access it that way.

Step Two: Gather Reinforcements

Ask some volunteers to come during the final ten minutes of class time to assist during checkout. They can help with general crowd control or be assigned to a child with special needs who requires individual supervision. Arrange for a volunteer to take kids with sensory sensitivities to the quiet room, or a quiet area, to be picked up. As kids get used to the checkout routine, fewer volunteers may be needed.

Step Three: Train the Kids

Go over the checkout process with the children during your first meeting. Make sure they know where to store papers and craft items, along with coats and jackets, so they can gather everything at checkout time. Practice lining up, sitting in a circle (or whatever you want them to do at checkout time), and checking out with you before they leave. Role play walking down the hall and out the door with parents. Begin the second session by reviewing how to check out and practice again if needed. Once checkout is going smoothly, conduct refresher courses when a tune-up is required.

Step Four: Stick to Protocol

You may feel inflexible sticking to the protocol, but it's there for a reason. If a child's registration says Dad or Mom will pick the child up, only release the child to Dad or Mom, even though Big Sister is very persuasive. Insist that kids hang up their coats and store crafts they want to take home in the same place each time. Don't dismiss class early. In other words, follow the protocol communicated by and to the parents. If the protocol undergoes a change, communicate with the parents before the change begins. If someone thinks checkout is too rigid, politely and persistently remind them that the process is in place for the safety of the children.

Step Five: Communicate

When a problem arises during checkout time, communicate as soon as possible with everyone involved. Talk to the children's ministry director, the special needs ministry director, the pastor, and the parents. Make them aware of potential problems and how to avoid them. Discuss changes that need to be made.

A smooth and safe checkout process is both a welcome guest and the perfect ending to children's ministry events. So add it to the guest list first and send it home last every single time.

Strategy 2—Draw What We Did

Kids live in the present. They are so skilled at reveling in right now, they often need to be coached to reflect upon what's been learned in the past—even if the past is fifteen short minutes ago. "Draw What We Did" is a quick and easy way to engage kids in the art of reflection and can be used as a wrap-up activity while kids wait to be picked up. And it gives parents a visual record to use as a conversation springboard for kids with communication delays.

"Draw What We Did" Basics

The basics of this strategy are easy and require only a few materials: blank paper and markers, crayons, or colored pencils. As dismissal time nears, give each child a piece of paper and have the drawing materials handy. Ask kids what they enjoyed, what the lesson was about, what games were played, and so on. As they answer, ask them to draw a picture about it.

If time allows, do a little role playing. Pretend to be the parent and point to a picture. Ask different children to tell you about their pictures. Coach them about what to say until they understand the process. When the parents arrive, encourage them to ask their children about the drawings, too.

"Draw What We Did" Variations

This very simple strategy is easy to spice up. These twists use the same materials and accommodate for the needs of kids at a variety of developmental levels.

- *Model the process.* Introduce this activity for the first time by modeling it. Think out loud about what happened and make simple drawings and stick figures on the whiteboard. Have a child role play the part of the parent and ask what you did. You play the part of the child and explain the drawings. Then instruct children to copy your drawings or create their own.
- *Fold the paper.* Fold and then unfold the paper into four sections. Have kids draw a picture in each section. For kids able to

fold their own papers, show and tell them to fold it in half hamburger-style to make a short, squat rectangle half. Or show and tell how to fold it hot-dog-style to make a long, skinnier rectangle. Use the same technique for the second fold, also.

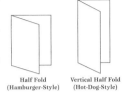

Half Fold
(Hamburger-Style)

Vertical Half Fold
(Hot-Dog-Style)

- *Draw as you go.* Fold the paper in four sections at the beginning of the session. At the end of four different activities, stop and have kids draw what they did.
- *Write a sentence.* Underneath each picture, have kids write a sentence about what they did.
- *Dictate a sentence.* Children who haven't learned to write yet, or write with difficulty, can dictate their sentence to someone else (you, a classroom assistant, or their buddy) who will write for them.
- *Card it.* Use the computer to preprint a brief summary of the day's lesson (the leader's manual may already have one) on one side of an index card. Have the kids draw a picture on the back side of the card.
- *Turn it around.* When parents come to pick up their kids, give them a blank piece of paper. Ask them to go home and draw what they did in their Sunday school class or at Bible study and share it with their child.

This strategy has special appeal to kids whose visual and spatial skills are stronger than their verbal skills. It gives every child one more way to process what was presented to them, and one more avenue God may choose to implant His truth into their young hearts.

Strategy 3—Short Video Options for Closing Time

Many children with disabilities are drawn to screens. Often, a small amount of screen time can enhance learning, provide a short respite from group activities, and calm anxieties at the end of class. Check out the list below for some products that might engage kids in your children's program as activities draw to a close.

- *Yancy:* Yancy, a songwriter and singer, creates music that appeals to kids and adults. Her DVDs, as well as CDs, can be purchased on her website. (www.yancynotnancy.com)

- *Kids Videos on GodTube:* If you have a room with Internet access, these videos can be viewed on a computer or a wireless device. The videos are free. (http://www.godtube.com)
- *Veggie Tales:* Phil Vischer and his team have created engaging, fun, and humorous videos that help teach Bible stories, as well as the meaning behind them. (www.veggietales.com)
- *What's in the Bible?:* By the creators of *Veggie Tales,* the *What's in the Bible?* series is a full curriculum offering kids a deep look at the context of our faith, and helping them to connect the themes that lead to salvation. While this is sold as a full curriculum, videos can be purchased individually. (www.whatsinthebible.com)
- *Ministry to Children Videos:* This site, created by veteran children's pastor Tony Kummer, contains thousands of great ideas, downloads, and resources. The videos on this site are free. (www.ministry-to-children.com)
- *Group Publishing:* Group Publishing creates curriculum, books, and other resources to enhance spiritual growth and development. Their videos can supplement teaching, and also encourage active participation that results in fun for all. (www.group.com)

Strategy 4—Music Cues for Easier Transitions

Transition times can be hard for kids to manage. Interrupt a three-year-old at play with the news it's time to go home and things can get ugly fast. Most kids get better at handling transitions from one activity to another as they get older. But kids on the autism spectrum or with developmental delays may find transitions stressful and unpleasant long after their age-mates have adapted.

What Kind of Music?

Music is a valuable tool to assist kids in transitioning from one activity to the next throughout children's ministry programs. Any kid-friendly music can be used. Sing a song, hum a melody, strum a guitar, play the piano, or turn on the CD player or iPod connected to speakers. Just make sure the music is appropriate for the situation, familiar, and closer to the calming/soothing side of the scale than to the rile-'em-up side.

How Can Music Cue a Transition?

Music can be used as a transition cue in a variety of situations. It can warn of an upcoming transition, announce the beginning of a transition, or indicate the length of time for an entire activity. But before using music to cue transitions, children must learn to recognize the cues, and have time to practice and become familiar with them. These strategies help them recognize the cues and show them how to respond.

Introduce song. Teach kids a simple song, review an old favorite, or play a CD. Give them time to learn the words and melody, or become familiar with the CD track before using it in any other way.

Explain the cue. Once kids are familiar with the song, explain that it is special because it is more than just a song. It is giving a message. Explain what the message is:

- When the song is over, it will be time to move on to something else.
- When the song begins, it is time to start something new.
- You can work on this activity from when the song starts until it ends. Then it will be time to transition.

Practice, practice, practice. Give children the opportunity to practice a few times. Watch to see if they understand what the music cue means. If not, explain it again and practice some more.

Introduce one music cue at a time. Stick with one music cue until the kids show they've got it down. When they do, introduce another one. But be careful. Like any good thing, the effectiveness wears off with overuse.

> ### Free Online Children's Ministry Music Resources
>
> http://childbiblesongs.com/
>
> http://www.jollynotes.com/
>
> http://childrensbiblesongs.us/

Keep the volume low. Some kids who have a hard time with transitions are also sensory sensitive. Loud music may overwhelm or agitate them. So keep the volume low and, as was mentioned before, select music that is soothing and calm.

Strategy 5—Learning Stations at Wrap-Up Time

When we think of teaching Sunday school, we think of teaching as an adult in front of the room, providing information. While listening to the teacher is certainly a way to learn about Jesus, kids can also learn through self-guided activities at learning stations. Often this can be more appealing to all kids, but especially those with special needs. Hands-on, self-paced activities allow kids to gather information in a different way.

Supplement Content with Learning Stations

Learning stations can supplement a teacher-led class, or become the primary way for kids to learn as they go from station to station. This largely depends upon the available space, materials and the strengths and needs of the children in the class. They also can be effective at reinforcing learning during wrap-up time. To create learning stations, consider the children in the classroom and the content you want them to learn.

Creative Learning Station Ideas

For example, if you are teaching about the life and ministry of Jesus, your learning stations would focus on information from the Gospels. Here are some ideas:

- *Sequencing cards* for stories about Jesus, like raising Lazarus from the dead.
- *A listening station* at which kids can use headphones and listen to stories from the Gospels.
- *A game station* at which kids can play a card game or board game that reinforces what they have learned about Jesus's life.
- *An art center* where children can make murals or books that retell what they have read or learned.
- *A drama corner* where kids can dress up and act out the stories.
- *A reading corner* where students who enjoy books can dive into more information.

While it is helpful to keep centers current and provide fresh activities, old favorites are always appropriate and welcome. Including previously taught content will reinforce what has been learned, and also can provide some predictability for kids who feel most comfortable with the familiar.

Teach Kids How to Use Learning Stations

When using learning stations in your program, remember to show children exactly how to do each activity so that they can be successful, careful, and safe with all of the materials. Allow them to practice how to behave and what to do in each station before starting, so they feel comfortable and ready. As you circulate to check on their understanding, redirect them, and encourage them, don't forget to enjoy them, too. Their insight may surprise you, and give you a new perspective on age-old truth.

Strategy 6—Calming Anxiety at Checkout Time

Excruciating. Children who live with anxiety may not know how to pronounce the word. But when they're waiting at church for their parents to pick them up, they know how excruciating feels. When they repeatedly ask questions like "When will Mom get here? What if Dad never comes? Do you think they were in an accident?" they are really asking you to calm their excruciating inner turmoil.

Be Proactive

Being proactive is a crucial component of calming an anxious child, and it begins when parents register kids for Sunday school or other programs. If parents mention that their children are anxious, call or email to learn more about how to calm their fears. If their child gets particularly worried when waiting at checkout time, ask for cell phone numbers to call if parents do run late. Creating a social story (see page 102) to read during checkout time might also be helpful. If anxiety issues surface as the year progresses, talk to the parents about how to handle them. For parents who are consistently late in picking up their children, clearly describe the level of the child's anxiety and stress the importance of being on time.

Be a Calming Presence

When a child becomes anxious, adults can do several things to be a calming presence and to model how to remain calm.

Acknowledge a child's feelings. Adults tend to diminish or dismiss fears that are very real to an anxious child. We say "There's nothing to worry about," or "Toughen up," or "Don't be a worry wart." No matter how often those phrases are used, the child will still be worried. So we might as well acknowledge it by saying things like, "It's hard to wait, isn't it?" or "I understand that you are wondering when Mom will pick you up," or "What's got you worried?"

Listen. Once you've acknowledged the child's struggle with anxiety, let him talk. Listen to what he has to say. Sometimes being heard is enough. And what a child says often gives clues about the best way to provide reassurance.

Offer comfort. When the child is done talking, or when what's being said is a rehash of what's already been said, offer comfort. The best way to comfort a child will vary depending on the situation, but here are some ideas:

- *Empathize and state the facts.* Say, "I understand that you are worried your Dad will forget to pick you up, but he remembered you every time so far." Or you could say, "You're worried because you're the last child waiting, but we were done early and your mom said her meeting wouldn't be over for five more minutes."
- *Make the anxiety wait.* Tell the child "I can tell you are really worried, and I'm glad you told me. Let's wait five minutes and if the worry is still there, we'll decide what to do about it then." Then set a visual timer (see page 101) and involve the child in a different activity until it rings.
- *Redirect the child.* Encourage the child to do something else—play a game, listen to music, read a book, or draw.
- *Take control of the situation.* If a child is truly panicked, take control of the situation by saying "I am going to take care of this. I will make sure that you find your mom and you will not get lost in the crowd."
- *Breathe deep.* When a child grows increasingly distressed, instruct him to take deep breaths in and out, in and out.
- *Call the parent.* Once a child needs deep breathing to remain calm, it's time to call Mom or Dad so they can assure him they are coming soon.

Employing these strategies tells children that they are understood and their feelings matter. When used consistently and compassionately, children learn to trust more and worry less so they can enjoy participating in church activities from beginning to the very, very end.

Strategy 7—Reassuring a Child Who Had a Difficult Time

I hate church and I am never coming back again.
No one here even likes me!

Despite our careful planning, some days are just rough for kids with disabilities. We can prepare our lessons, offer choices, create attractive activities, and set up our rooms to be welcoming and comfortable. We can even read books or attend workshops to help us understand the kids we serve. Still, some days are difficult.

Respond Compassionately

It is important to remember that the children in your group may have had a difficult time before they arrived at church. Perhaps a sibling ate the last Pop-Tart®, or took an extra turn on the Wii™. It could be that his favorite shirt is in the laundry, or she couldn't find the quarters she wanted to put in the offering basket. Kids might be tired, worried about a test in school, or just plain out-of-sorts. While kids who are typically developing may participate fully in their Sunday school group despite these distractions, those who have disabilities may not be able to settle in and enjoy the lesson. Unfortunately, these difficulties can result in frustration that leads to anger, tears, and sadness. Kids might break class rules or refuse to participate.

Speak Reassuringly

At the end of the lesson, these children may feel remorse. They also might be concerned about the consequences of their behavior; they may realize that their parents will be told what has transpired during church, or they may become embarrassed that their peers have seen them make poor choices. Whatever their reaction, we have an incredible opportunity to demonstrate grace and offer comfort. Consider a conversation like this:

> *Child:* I *hate* church and I am *never* coming back again. No one here even likes me!
> *Teacher:* Today has been a hard day, hasn't it?
> *Child:* Yes, and I am *never* coming back.
> *Teacher:* You aren't coming back?
> *Child: No!* Because I am being bad and no one likes me.
> *Teacher:* No one likes you?
> *Child:* Well, we are supposed to obey and *God doesn't like me.*
> *Teacher:* It has really been a hard morning. We all have mornings like that. I know I do. When we have a rough time at church, here is what we do. We help each other calm down and we clean up. You are really calm now. Can you help me pick up these blocks?
> *Child:* Okay.
> *Teacher:* Great! After that, let's write a note to Tommy. He was sad when the blocks got knocked over. But I know that he will forgive you. That is what we do in our class. And God will always forgive you, too.

Listen Reflectively

By listening reflectively to what the child is saying, and by offering matter-of-fact truth and comfort, this teacher helped the child to process the events of the day. It is important to note that the child's behavior was not excused because of the disability, but the teacher approached the situation in a respectful, direct way. The teacher guided the child to move toward forgiveness and reconciliation. This is an important lesson, not only for the child with disabilities, but also for the other kids, teachers, and parents as well.

Strategy 8—What's Coming Up Next Time?

Kids are curious, and they like to anticipate and imagine what could happen next. So at the end of class, while the kids are waiting to be collected by their families, why not tap into their curiosity and talk about what's happening next time?

Preview the Menu

When class ends with talk about what will happen next time, at least three good things happen. A sneak peek at next week builds anticipation. That anticipation creates motivation to return next week. Imagine having a parent suggest the family skip church and having a child respond, "But my teacher said we're going to live in the belly of a whale like Jonah this morning. I have to be there!" Could a parent say *no* to that?

But talking about what will happen next time does more than build anticipation. It can reduce anxiety in worry-prone kids. Also, giving kids a peek at next week's topic is a way to front-load their brains. They can contemplate the tidbit of information received, be alert to related concepts or situations, and come back next week with minds already focused on the upcoming topic of discussion.

How to Talk about Next Time

What's happening next time can be introduced in many different ways, depending on what you want the discussion to accomplish.

To motivate kids to return, make the discussion exciting. Haul out an unusual prop or costume and ask kids how they think it will be used. Offer clues and invite them to return to solve the mystery. Display a few intriguing photographs or pictures and promise to reveal the whole story next time.

To reduce anxiety, provide a visual schedule (see page 40) for children to look at and review. Or, if next time will be quite out of the ordinary, create and read a social story about how to adjust to changes at Sunday school or midweek events. If possible, let the kids take the schedule or social story home to review with parents throughout the week.

To front-load the brain, give kids a snippet of information and encourage them to think about it. Ask what they think about the information they've been given: "What could fishing have to do with the Bible? Why do you think you need to put on your dancing shoes for next week?" Or use the snippet to introduce a game of Twenty Questions.

The sneak peek strategy can transform a session wrap-up from waiting-to-go-home time into I-can't-wait-to-come-again-next-week time. And where eager souls are waiting, Jesus loves to do His work.

We all hate to be the bearers of bad tidings don't we? Delivering difficult news can be uncomfortable for everyone. However, good communication is necessary in church families. When communicating with parents about behavioral incidents, we need to choose our words carefully so that we can be allies rather than adversaries. This ultimately supports the spiritual growth of the child. In the next section, you'll read about how to report accurately while maintaining a relationship that honors the family and Christ.

Strategy 9—Communication, Part 1: Communicating with Parents at Pick-Up Time

It's been a tough morning in your class. Janey arrived in a bad mood, which quickly became an angry tantrum. She calmed fairly quickly, but not before tearing up some of the craft materials and overturning a chair. Although you and your assistant teacher kept Janey and her classmates safe, you now need to let Janey's parents know what has transpired.

Show Grace to Tired Parents

Parents of kids with disabilities are accustomed to difficult news. Their week might include arguing with insurance companies about denied claims, or learning that the best speech therapist in town is not taking new patients. They might also receive calls about misbehavior at school, or meltdowns at Scouts or T-ball. Still, learning about a difficult time at Sunday school can be upsetting. After all, Sunday is supposed to be a day of rest, and many parents wish that their child's disability would just take a day off.

Three Ways to Speak with Grace

With this in mind, we need to be cautious and caring as we discuss behavioral incidents. Consider the following tips for making these conversations grace-filled and productive.

- *Accentuate the positive.* While it might have been a difficult morning, identify at least one positive aspect of the child's time with you. For example, start with "Hi, Mrs. Lewis! How was your Bible class? We've had a busy day here. I was so impressed that Janey remembered her contribution to the mission project. She was one of the only kids who brought in a book for the kids at the shelter. I love her caring heart."
- *Find a quiet space to talk.* Remember that parents often feel judged within the Christian community; they worry that others perceive their child's disability as a result of bad parenting. Therefore, when reporting about a child's behavior, try to find a place where you can be sure others are not listening.
- *Describe what you heard and what you saw.* It's natural to want to vent your frustration about a child's behavior, but this is not the time. As you describe what happened, use words that depict what you heard and saw; do not describe your opinions or feelings about the incident.
- *Offer reassurance.* After hearing your description, parents might be embarrassed, sad, angry, or overwhelmed. Take time to reassure them that you understand, and that you want to help.

Instead, Try This

So, instead of this....

> Janey walked into the room with a mean look on her face. She took one look at the project we were going to do and she screamed and yelled so loud that I couldn't hear myself think. She walked right over to the art table and tore apart the construction paper and then pushed over a chair. Then she stomped over to the reading area in a huff and just ignored our directions. It sure took a long time for her to get herself together, but finally she did. I don't usually see behavior like that in a third grader!

Try this...

> When Janey arrived this morning, she appeared angry; her eyebrows were furrowed and her arms were crossed. When she saw we were making cards for the pastors, she yelled, "I hate making cards and I'm not

going to do it." She ripped up some papers and pushed over a chair. After that, she walked over to the reading corner and sat quietly. She didn't respond to our invitations to join the circle, but after about fifteen minutes, she walked over and joined us. The rest of the class time went just fine, and she seems very calm now.

Some days can be like this. I really do understand. This won't be the last time someone in our class has a bad day. I will tell you, though, that I can't imagine our class without Janey. She is such an important part of our group. Please let me know if there is anything I can do to make days like this easier. Also, please know that I just can't wait to see her next week.

Good communication takes time and practice, but it's worth the effort. Our words are powerful!

Strategy 10—Communication, Part 2: Communicating with Other Volunteers About Kids' Behavior

Picture this: three Sunday school volunteers, gathered in the hallway after Sunday school. Volunteer 1 works in the third grade room. Volunteers 2 and 3 work in the fifth grade room. Let's listen in on their conversation:

Volunteer 1: Have you seen Mrs. Cooper's third grader? He sure is in a bratty mood today.

Volunteer 2: I know. And I heard that her preschool child knows some VERY colorful words. She is really mean to the other kids in the room, too. She's a handful. At least that's what I heard.

Volunteer 3: Oh, are you talking about the Cooper kids? Wow. They're headed for trouble when they're teenagers.

Volunteer 1: Yeah. Mrs. Cooper told the pastor that the third grader takes *(lower voice to a whisper)* medication for controlling anxiety. I'm only telling you that so you'll pray for them. Don't tell anyone else.

Volunteer 3: Oh, of course. Mrs. Cooper is really challenged by those kids.

Volunteer 2: Bless her heart.

What's Wrong with This Communication?

Think for a moment. What's wrong with this conversation? If you answered *just about everything,* please give yourself a gold star, a pat on the back, and a piece of dark chocolate. Here is a summary of the problems:

- The conversation takes place in a public area of the church.
- Only one volunteer works directly with the Cooper children.
- Volunteer 1 is spreading information given to a pastor.
- Words like "bratty" and "mean" are not edifying.
- The conversation focuses solely on the perceived problems.
- The whole conversation is gossip.
- The gossip is wrapped up in Christianese—*pray for her* and the tagline *bless her heart*—that is supposed to make it acceptable.

What if Mrs. Cooper, or one of her children had overheard this? What is the likelihood that they might return to church?

How to Encourage Good Communication

Good communication requires thought and effort. We need to choose our words carefully, with the goals of maintaining safety, improving our teaching and behavior management abilities, and nurturing the child's and family's spiritual growth.

We encourage each church to develop some guidelines for communication that will edify the body of Christ while maintaining the dignity and confidentiality of each family. A confidentiality document (see Appendix D, page 171) is one way to communicate this policy to volunteers and family members.

Confidentiality breeds respect and trust—foundational elements of any relationship.

Strategy 11—Communication, Part 3: Communicating via Social Media

Let's pretend for a moment. After a busy day, you sit down on your comfy couch and eagerly log into Facebook. You're ready for a little mindless surfing, and perhaps a turn or two of Words with Friends. You scroll down your news feed and notice a church friend's status update:

> OMG...I cannot BELIEVE people still drive MINI-VANS. Seriously...have you never heard of SUVs? Why

not just get a sign that says, "My life is over! I drive a VAN?!" #minivansaretheworst

You feel your face flush with embarrassment as you glance at the driveway, where your slightly dented, yet reliable minivan is parked. That would be so mortifying and hurtful, wouldn't it?

Imagine if the friend weren't talking about your minivan, though. Imagine if she were talking about your child.

> Can anyone help me? I have this kid in my Sunday school class who has the worst behavior . . . it's so distracting. He talks constantly about things that are of no interest to any of the kids, and he doesn't even realize it. I feel so bad for his mom. Any suggestions?

Believe it or not, these kinds of things happen.

Proactive Planning for Positive Communication

Communication, now more than ever, takes careful, proactive planning. We're constantly connected—wirelessly—to each other, and information spreads quickly. Please note that we didn't say *truth* spreads quickly. The information that is shared online, through texts and, of course, in conversations can be forwarded and repeated hundreds of times before an error or miscommunication is caught.

Acronym for Positive Communication

In order to protect our students, consider this acronym for positive communication via social media. Before you speak or post or text or email, think, *Is it . . .*

T=True
H=Helpful
I=Important
N=Necessary
K=Kind

We all make mistakes with our words. However, when we *think* before we speak, we protect the children—and parents—we serve.

Chapter 10

To-Go Box: Bible Activities for Families to Enjoy at Home

Which supper gets your vote—a gourmet dinner prepared by friends at their home or a take-out meal on the road? Uh-huh. All other things being equal, the gourmet meal wins hands down. But, all things are not always equal. Sometimes, extra duties at work, family commitments, illness, and unexpected events crowd out gourmet dinners or even a home-cooked meal. The stomach starts growling and suddenly, a to-go box from the deli down the street sounds delicious.

Even children who want to come to church can't always make it. Sometimes their absences are due to challenges like illness, a death in the family, car trouble, or bad weather. Sometimes they're due to happy events like a new baby, a birthday celebration, or vacation. Whatever the reason, when children have to miss regular church events, their young hearts get hungry. Their awakening spirits need to be fed. Even though spiritual food tastes best when served with a side of fellowship, a to-go box full of activities to feed the soul can keep a heart from grumbling.

Consider this final chapter of *Every Child Welcome* to be a take-home menu for kids who either can't always attend children's ministry activities, or as something to snack on throughout the week. You'll find instructions for creating travel totes and for sending home books or videos from the church library. Resources like these are valuable for all children. But for children with health-related special needs, they may be an essential component of their spiritual training and fitness.

A Prayer of Commissioning

Lord, please be with the children who are absent this week. May these take-home resources satisfy their hunger for You. May the activities, books, movies, and websites teach children more about who You are. By Your power, heal young bodies and intervene in circumstances so children return again next time and feast on You.

Strategy 1—Travel Totes

Vacations and holiday visits to Grandma's house are meant to be fun. While most families look forward to their time away from home, these trips can present challenges for families affected by disabilities. Changes in routine can cause anxiety and fatigue. Children with sensory issues may struggle with changes in temperature or bedding. The experience of flying on a plane can be overwhelming, as can the prospect of sitting for long hours in the family van.

We can't solve all of these issues, of course. However, we can help to make these trips easier by providing some activities for kids to do during the trip. This is an easy, cost-effective, practical way to demonstrate love for families.

To create travel totes, find inexpensive gift bags or use brown paper grocery bags. Fill these with small items that will engage kids, and also remind them of their church family. Items can include:

- Coloring sheets from your curriculum or from Ministry to Children (www.ministry-to-children.com)
- Small notebooks for drawing or writing
- Stress or squishy toys
- Small picture or story books
- Travel games
- Psalm 121, written on an index card
- Stickers

This is a small gesture. However, parents in these families will be grateful for your kindness. By taking time to prepare these totes, you will be communicating that you understand that travel can be difficult. Your willingness to consider this, and attempt to make their journey easier is a tremendous investment in your relationship with these families. Bon Voyage!

Add Reading Material to the Travel Tote

In addition to the items listed above, consider tucking these into the tote, too:

- *Autograph books.* Kids can use these to get autographs from relatives and friends. It's a great way to help them socialize and remember who they met.
- *A letter from you.* Wish children a great trip, with the promise that you will be excited to see them when they return.
- *A social story.* About taking a trip, of course.
- *A travel journal.* To share with you upon their return.

Strategy 2—Library To-Go Bags

Kids with special needs benefit when what was presented at church activities is reinforced throughout the week. Many church libraries need to make the congregation aware of the materials and services they offer. Both those needs can be met by sending library to-go bags home with children who are part of your special needs ministry.

What Are Library To-Go Bags?

Library to-go bags are similar in many ways to the vacation travel totes described previously. But they differ in a few crucial ways. Vacation totes are stocked with consumable resources, but library to-go bags contain books and videos to be returned and recirculated. Therefore, library bags are supposed to be checked out and returned every week or two so other families of kids with special needs can use them.

What's the Bag Like?

To-go bags can be as simple or as elaborate as the budget and time allows. If there's a seamstress in the congregation willing to sew cloth bags, do that. Or order clear plastic bags with handles from a library supply catalog. If money is tight, purchase plastic zipper bags in different sizes from the grocery store. A pocket for a due-date reminder card is nice, but not essential.

What Should Be in a To-Go Bag?

Determining what to put in to-go bags should be a cooperative venture between the children's ministry volunteer who wants to launch the project and the library staff. To-go bags can be stocked with whatever age-appropriate items the library offers—books, videos, audiobooks, puppets—with the selections made in light of concepts recently presented. One or two items per bag is plenty.

How Are the To-Go Bags Managed?

If the church library already has a checkout process, use it. Otherwise, create your own checkout system. All that's needed is a notebook for recording the contents of each bag, who took it home and when it is due, along with a card indicating when the bag should be returned. Once your checkout system is in place, send home one bag per child per week. Wait to distribute the bag until checkout time when the parent arrives so the due date and the contents of the bag can be reviewed together. Let the parents and child know that more bags are available for checkout in the future, but only one at a time, to up the chances of the to-go bag being returned.

What If a Bag Doesn't Come Back?

Some bags won't be returned. That's a given. So before launching the ministry, talk to the church library staff for advice about what their policy is. Discuss how much can be written off as a ministry expense, and when it's appropriate to ask for a donation to replace an item. You may even consider finding a sponsor who is willing to underwrite replacement losses.

Always remember that the book, or video, or Bible character puppet that isn't returned might be spreading the good news of the gospel in a home where it's never been heard before instead of sitting unused in the church library. Those materials are feeding hungry souls instead of leaving the lost hungry for more. Sounds like one more way to fulfill the Great Commission, doesn't it?

Conclusion

Earlier we said we hoped this book would become like a well-worn cookbook on your kitchen shelf, with the pages dog-eared and your notes scrawled in the margins. That kind of transformation is accomplished through time and practice and hard work. The beginning stages of the process often feel overwhelming and exhausting. Who knows? You might be feeling that way right now. And that's an okay place to be in the beginning.

But it's not a good place to stay for very long. When those feelings creep in, we invite you to take a break and see what's cooking at our blogs. Jolene serves special needs parenting and ministry encouragement at www.DifferentDream.com, and Katie whips up delightful resources for families, churches, and schools at www.KatieWetherbee.com. So grab a cup of coffee and pull up a chair. We'd love to sit down and chat with you.

We also conduct onsite special needs ministry training workshops around the country. If your church or a consortium of churches in your area is interested in hosting a special needs ministry training, contact either Jolene or Katie. We'd love to meet you in person.

Resources

Special Needs Products

Special Needs Companies
- Therapro, Inc.: www.therapro.com
- The Therapy Shoppe: www.therapyshoppe.com

Specific Products
- Colored overlays: http://www.amazon.com/IRLEN-Colored-Overlays-Reading-Sample/dp/B003LNMHTU
- Florescent light filters: http://www.educationalinsights.com/search.do?query=classroom+light+filters
- Highlighter strips: http://www.enasco.com/c/reading/Teacher+Resources/ Highlighter+Strips/?ref=breadcrumb
- Kids' Horizontal Bible Tabs: http://www.christianbook.com/kids-horizontal-bible-tabs/pd/105080
- Post-It Tabs: http://www.post-it.com/wps/portal/3M/en_US/PostItNA/Home/Products/~/Post-it/Tabs/?N=5927572+4327&rt=r3
- Visual Timers: www.timetimer.com
- Wee Sing Bible Songs: http://weesing.com/Books-Music/Wee-Sing-Bible-Songs

Teaching Resources and Sample Activities

Visual Schedules

- Boardmaker Software: http://www.mayer-johnson.com/board-maker-software
- Tips for making visual schedules: http://challengingbehavior.fmhi.usf.edu/explore/pbs_docs/tips_for_visuals.pdf
- Visual Schedule Ideas on Pinterest: www.pinterest.com/aacandat/visual-schedules/
- Visual Schedules: http://www.gvsu.edu/cms3/assets/2CF6CA25-D6C6-F19E-339DC5CD2EB1B543/secondarylevellinkprograms/visual_schedules.docx
- Downloadable Visuals: http://connectability.ca/visuals-engine/

Easy-to-Make Gifts

- Christmas: http://www.ivillage.ca/parenting/easy-crafts-kids/homemade-christmas-gifts and http://www.parentmap.com/article/15-homemade-christmas-gifts-that-kids-can-make
- Mother's Day: http://www.buzzfeed.com/donnad/easy-emergency-mothers-day-crafts-for-kids
- Father's Day: http://www.parenting.com/gallery/7-easy-to-make-gifts-for-fathers-day

Social Stories

- Kids Can Dream: http://kidscandream.webs.com/page12.htm
- Sensory Processing Disorder Pinterest page: http://www.pinterest.com/sensoryprocessi/social-stories/
- Spectronics Blog: http://www.spectronics.com.au/blog/tools-and-resources/tips-for-creating-successful-social-stories/
- The Watson Institute downloadable behavior stories: www.thewatsoninstitute.org/
- Vanderbilt University: http://csefel.vanderbilt.edu/resources/strategies.html

Miscellaneous

- Bible Pronunciation Guide: http://netministries.org/Bbasics/bwords.htm
- Let Me Introduce Myself: katiewetherbee.files.wordpress.com/2012/02/keystudentintro.docx
- Responsive Classroom Website: https://www.responsiveclassroom.org/

- Role Playing Skits: http://www.kidssundayschool.com/14/gradeschool/skits.php and http://www.kidssundayschool.com/14/gradeschool/skits.php?start=m&end=n

Special Needs Ministry Team Tools
- Background check service: www.protectmyministry.com
- *The Church and Disability: The Weblog Disabled Christianity*; Jeff McNair (CreateSpace, 2010)
- Confidentiality and Respect Guidelines: katiewetherbee.files.wordpress.com/2012/01/keyconfidentialityguidelines.docx
- *Exceptional Teaching: A Comprehensive Guide for Including Students with Disabilities;* Jim Pierson (Standard Publishing Company, 2002)
- Grow Plan for Spiritual Development: katiewetherbee.files.wordpress.com/2012/02/keyringgrowplan.docx
- Inclusion Ministry Covenant: http://katiewetherbee.com/2012/01/26/communication-and-confidentiality-building-trust/
- Ministry to Children: www.ministry-to-children.com
- Misunderstood Minds (PBS): www.pbs.org/wgbh/misunderstoodminds/writingdiffs.html
- *Same Lake, Different Boat: Coming alongside People Touched by Disability*; Stephanie Hubach (P & R Publishing, 2006)
- *Special Needs, Special Ministry*; Joni Eareckson-Tada (Group Publishing, 2003)

Books
For Children
- *Don't Call Me Special: A First Look at Disability*; Pat Thomas (Barron's Educational Series, 2005) Preschool & up
- *Ellie Bean the Drama Queen: A Children's Book About Sensory Processing Disorder*; Jennie Harding (Sensory World, 2011)
- *A Friend Like Simon*; Kate Gaynor (Special Stories Publishing, 2009) Autism Spectrum Disorder
- *In Jesse's Shoes: Appreciating Kids with Special Needs*; Beverly Lewis (Bethany House, 2007) Primary & up
- *Just the Way I Am: God's Good Design in Disability*; Krista Horning (Christian Focus Publications, 2011)
- *My Brother Charlie*; Holly Robinson Peete (Scholastic Press, 2010) 2nd–5th

- *My Friend Isabelle*; Eliza Woloson (Woodbine House, 2013) Down Syndrome
- *Special People, Special Ways*; Arlene Maguire (Future Horizons, 2000) Kindergarten & up
- *Susan Laughs*; Jeanne Willis and Tony Ross (Henry Holt and Co, 2000) Preschool–2nd
- *Thank You, Mr Falker*; Patricia Polacco (Philomel, 2012) Kindergarten & up

For Older Children
- *Window Boy*; Andrea White (Bright Sky Press, 2008) Cerebral Palsy
- *Small Steps: The Year I Got Polio*; Peg Kehret (Albert Whitman & Co., 1996)

For Adults
- *Autism and Your Church: Nurturing the Spiritual Growth of People with Autism Spectrum Disorder*; Barbara J. Newman (Faith Alive Christian Resources, 2011)
- *A Different Dream for My Child: Meditations for Parents of Critically or Chronically Ill Children*; Jolene Philo (Discovery House Publishers, 2009)
- *Different Dream Parenting: A Practical Guide to Raising a Child with Special Needs*; Jolene Philo (Discovery House Publishers, 2011)
- *A Good and Perfect Gift: Faith, Expectations, and a Little Girl Named Penny*; Amy Julia Becker (Bethany House, 2011)
- *Uncommon Beauty: Crisis Parenting from Day One*; Margaret Meder (Beaver's Pond Press, 2012)
- *Unexpected Journey: When Special Needs Change Our Course;* Cindi and Joe Ferrini (Morris Publishing, 2009)

Special Needs Ministry Websites and Resources
- Chosen Families: http://chosenfamilies.org/
- CLC Network: www.clcnetwork.org
- Different Dream: http://www.differentdream.com/
- Diving for Pearls: http://katiewetherbee.com/
- The Inclusive Church: http://theinclusivechurch.wordpress.com/
- Insight for Living Special Needs Ministry: http://insightforliving.typepad.com/specialneeds/

- Joni and Friends: www.joniandfriends.org
- Key Ministry: http://www.keyministry.org/
- Not Alone: http://specialneedsparenting.net/
- P.U.R.E. Ministries: www.pure-ministries.com
- Snappin' Ministries: www.snappin.org
- Special Friends Ministry: http://specialneedsministry.wordpress.com/
- Standard Publishing Heart Shapers Curriculum: http://heartshaper.com/
- The Works of God Displayed: http://www.theworksofgoddisplayed.com/

Online Resources for Children's Ministries and Kids
Short Videos
- Group Publishing: http://www.group.com/
- Kids videos on God Tube: http://www.godtube.com/
- Ministry to Children Videos: www.ministry-to-children.com
- Veggie Tales: www.veggietales.com
- What's in the Bible: www.whatsinthebible.com
- Yancy: www.yancynotnancy.com

Music
- Child Bible Songs: http://childbiblesongs.com
- Children's Bible Songs: http://childrensbiblesongs.us
- Jolly Notes: www.jollynotes.com

Websites
- Adventures in Odyssey: www.whitsend.org
- Answers in Genesis: www.answersingenesis.org
- Bible Rhymes: www.biblerhymes.com
- Calvary Williamsport: www.calvarywilliamsport.com
- KidExplorers: http://www.christiananswers.net/kids
- Christian Kids Top 100 Sites: www.christiankidstop100.com
- Clubhouse Magazine: www.clubhousemagazine.com
- Coloring Pages For U: www.coloringpages4u.com/bible_coloringpages
- DJ TV Club: www.djtvclub.com
- Faith Girlz: www.faithgirlz.com
- Focus on the Family Radio Theater: http://www.focusonthefamily.com/radio-theatre
- Fun Bible Activities: www.funbibleactivities.com

- Grace Place Kids: http://graceplacekids.com
- Guide Magazine: www.guidemagazine.org
- His Kids: http://hiskids.net/
- JC Playzone: www.jcplayzone.com/Index.asp
- Kid Builder: http://kidbuilder.net
- A Kid's Heart: www.akidsheart.com/threer/lvl1/lvl1.htm
- Looky Lamb: www.lookylamb.org
- Wonder Zone: www.wonderzone.com

Appendix A

Special Needs
Ministry Covenant

The Rights and Responsibilities of Our Church Family

Parents have a *right* to:
- Communicate with the children's ministry staff.
- Enroll their child in Christian education that is safe, nurturing, and in line with our church's belief statement.
- Identify and use their gifts to serve the church.
- Learn about Christ and His plan for the family.

Parents have a *responsibility* to:
- Provide thorough and complete information related to the child's medical, behavioral, emotional, and spiritual strengths and needs.
- Remain at church during Sunday programming, and provide contact information during special programming.
- Understand that the church does not provide individual behavioral, academic, or language therapies.
- Participate in problem-solving that is productive and Christ-honoring.

Church staff/volunteers have a *right* to:
- Expect honesty and respect from parents.
- Expect honesty and respect from children.
- Serve in a safe environment.
- Grow in Christ through their service.

Church staff/volunteers have a *responsibility* to:
- Provide a Christian education that is safe, nurturing and in line with our church's belief statement.
- Thoroughly read parents' information about their child.
- Keep information about children's needs confidential.
- Participate in problem-solving that is productive and Christ-honoring.

Children have a *right* to:
- Learn about Jesus in a safe, nurturing environment.
- Receive reasonable support for academic, behavioral, medical, or social/emotional needs.
- Discover the gifts God has given them.
- Use those gifts in the church body.

Children have a *responsibility* to:
- Use words and actions that show respect to teachers and leaders at church.
- Treat other students kindly.
- Demonstrate safe behavior.
- Do their best work.

Appendix B

Let Me Introduce Myself

In my child's words...

My hopes and dreams are...

The hardest things for me at school and church are...

I wish my teachers would...

If I were in charge, I would...

My teachers help me the most by...

The best thing about school/church is...

It would be good if the other kids knew these things about me...

Appendix C

"Looks Like, Sounds Like, Feels Like" Chart

Looks Like	Sounds Like	Feels Like

Appendix D

Guidelines for Respect and Confidentiality

*Let the words of my mouth and the meditation of my heart
be acceptable in your sight, O LORD, my rock and my
redeemer. Psalm 19:14*

Respect and Confidentiality in Meetings, Face-to-Face Conversations, and on the Phone

- *Who:* Volunteers directly involved, supervising church staff, parents

- *What:* Information related to a child's behavior or interactions during church programming

- *When:* At a mutually agreeable time for all, keeping in mind that some incidents must be reported as soon as possible

- *Where:* In a location that is private enough to avoid others overhearing; NOT in a public restaurant or in a church hallway

- *Why:* To share information that will improve safety, provide insight and support the child's growth in church programming

- *How:* By reporting *facts*, not opinions, in an honest and kind way

Respect and Confidentiality in Emails

- *Who:* Church staff, volunteers, parents

- *What:* Information related to a child's behavior or interactions during church programming

- *When:* As needed to provide information that will be helpful to the volunteers and to the family

- *Where:* From individual's home computers or from church computers

- *Why:* To share information that will improve safety, provide insight, and support the child's growth in church programming

- *How:* Volunteers may send emails to church staff; church staff is directly responsible for email communication to families

Respect and Confidentiality on the Web

- *Who:* Church staff, volunteers, parents

- *What:* Information related to a child's behavior or interactions during church programming

- *When:* Scheduled online training, Skype conversations, when on social networking sites

- *Where:* Social networking sites such as Ning sites, Facebook, Google+; those logged in should be in a place where others cannot read over their shoulders or hear conversations

- *Why:* For training purposes, for problem-solving

- *How*: On the web, church staff, and volunteers should refrain from using children's full names. (Use initials, first names, or hypothetical situations.) Communication should be directly related to problem-solving and brainstorming and should be so respectful and kind that the communication about a specific child could be copied to parents for their review and participation. This communication should not be shared with anyone who is not directly involved in the ministry.